Midnight Marquee Number 77

Editors
Gary J. Svehla
Susan Svehla

Graphic Design Interior
Gary J. Svehla

Cover Design
Susan Svehla

Copy Editor
Susan Svehla

Contributing Writers
Anthony Ambrogio; Doug Lemoreux;
Arthur Lundquist; Cindy Collins Smith;
Brian Smith; Gary J. Svehla;
Steven Thornton

Acknowledgments
Warner Home Video; Fox Home Video; Universal Home Video;
Bender Helper Publicity; Scott Essman;

Publisher
Midnight Marquee Press, Inc.

Midnight Marquee
Number 77
March 2010
Copyright 2010 © by Gary J. Svehla

Published irregularly for $10 per issue by Midnight Marquee Press, Inc.

Articles and art should be transmitted electronically and will remain the property of the writer/artist and copyright holder, who will retain the rights. If material intended for publication is sent to us via regular mail, it is the sender's responsibility to include return postage. No responsibility is taken for unsolicited material.

Editorial views expressed by writers are not necessarily those of the publisher, Midnight Marquee Press. Nothing from the magazine may be reproduced or shared in any media without the expressed written permission of the publisher. The Midnight Marquee Press offices are located at: 9721 Britinay Lane, Parkville, MD 21234; website: http://www.midmar.com; e-mail: midmargary@aol.com

Letters of comment addressed to Midnight Marquee or Susan and Gary Svehla will be considered for publication, unless the writer requests otherwise.

Letters of comment are encouraged; please send all comments to midmargary@aol.com and label your comments "Comments for *MidMar* #77."

We are always looking for new writers to submit articles. Please discuss any article suggestions first with Gary J. Svehla at midmargary@aol.com and check the Style Sheet link on our website to get ideas for style and formatting. Length of articles may vary. We take them long and short. But remember, our emphasis is mainly on the classics of the Golden Age, but our definition of classic and Golden Age is not based upon specific decades or year of production necessarily, but upon the artistic content that reflects the heart and style of early horror cinema.

Copies are mailed, within the USA, for the cost of the issue plus $6 for Media Mail; $10 for Priority Mail. Issues are sent in sturdy mailers, so they should arrive at your home in near mint condition. Foreign orders are welcome, but shipping costs vary. Check with us. We accept all credit cards, PayPal and money orders.

TABLE OF CONTENTS

2   **Midnight Marquee Editorial**
         by Gary J. Svehla

3   ***The Invisible Man:***
         Forum/Against 'Em
         edited by Anthony Ambrogio

12   ***The Deadly Mantis*:**
         A Lot of Bug on a Little Budget
         by Doug Lemoreux

22   ***Midnight Marquee*** **Book Reviews**

24   ***Midnight Marquee*** **DVD Reviews**
         by Gary J. Svehla

Midnight Marquee Editorial

Welcome to the new format *Midnight Marquee*, now with fewer pages, but with higher quality paper and full-color reproduction on every page. We plan to publish more frequently because of this smaller format and hopefully can return to our twice a year publishing schedule.

After experimenting with digital online publishing, our readership made its voice heard, loud and clear, that they wanted a magazine they could hold in their hands, flip through, sniff the printer's ink and thrill at finding in their mailbox when they least expected it! We will try to maintain a hard print format for as long as we can, if the readers support this magazine format.

We want to say goodbye to two friends, one an icon of monster kids everywhere. Forrest J Ackerman, the founder of horror film fandom and *Famous Monsters of Filmland* magazine, passed away in 2009 after a long battle with health problems, but as long as people celebrate horror, science fiction and fantasy movies, Forry Ackerman shall *not* die. Never the perfect human being (who is?), he was always the perfect iconic mentor and educator of the bat pack brigade, teaching us about the cinematic treasures of the past, as well as introducing us to the not-so-classic product of the present. Forry was always kind, giving and patient, a true teacher, even if he never earned the academic credentials. Ever since I met the man in the mid-1960s at LunaCon, he was an inspiration to me, and I will miss his wicked sense of humor and support. He bought the very first copy of my magazine in 1963 and encouraged me to keep it going, if even sporadically, for 46-plus years. This magazine remains a living testament to his vision.

Sadly, *Midnight Marquee* staff member, friend and contributor, Delbert Winans, a celebrated (former) member of "the Baltimore boys," a loose community of horror buffs and memorabilia collectors, who visited one another's collections frequently, most often to admire new acquisitions and suggest a trade or two, passed away much too young. My mother Ann called Del "Mister Five-by-Five," based upon a song of her youth. Del was short but substantial in stature, a smile on his moon-face that lit up the room. Del was the life of the party, constantly chewing gum and talking a mile a minute, a true local raconteur. When his marriage disintegrated and Del needed space to heal, he followed his dreams, moved to the West Coast, and tried for the remainder of his life to get his idea of a horror film theme restaurant off the ground. Such was not to be, but he lived his dream until the very end. Unfortunately, by the time Del's health started to fail, we had drifted apart. But I always held a special place in my heart for Delbert and thought of him often.

This issue, *Midnight Marquee* #77, offers two feature articles. One a "Forum/Against 'Em" analysis of the James Whale Universal classic *The Invisible Man*, with many arguing it remains the best film that Whale directed and features the best use of humor in classic horror cinema. Unfortunately, I argue that the film is the most overrated of the classic Universal canon and that its overuse of special effects and silly humor ruins what could have been the classic horror movie that many people consider it to be. And secondly, to add a contrasting 1950s touch, we feature a detailed analysis of *The Deadly Mantis* that makes the strong case that this generally disparaged or ignored giant bug epic is one of the finest examples of the genre. And yes, we have oodles of DVD and book reviews to fill out the remainder of the issue. Next issue Anthony Ambrogio takes a close look at Ridley Scott's *Alien*. Your email comments are always appreciated!

—Gary J. Svehla

FORUM/AGAINST 'EM

Claude RAINS in THE INVISIBLE MAN

EDITED BY ANTHONY AMBROGIO

When it comes to invisible men, the stalwart individuals who make up the loose-knit online group known as "Fanexians" don't always see eye to eye. As always, editor Gary J. Svehla has definite ideas about an acknowledged Universal classic—ideas that put him at loggerheads with frequent *Midnight Marquee* contributors Steven Thornton, Brian Smith, Arthur Lundquist and Anthony Ambrogio. Female fellow contributor Cindy Collins Smith elaborates upon her own problems with *The Invisible Man*, and the usually loquacious Mark Clark limits himself to a couple of supporting comments this time around.

Gary: *The Invisible Man* (1933) is the most overpraised movie in the Universal canon. Except for its opening sequences, the film leaves me totally cold.

Steven: Excuse me, Mr. Publisher. But I remember someone writing in these pages, not too long ago, "I just want people to say in a public forum that *The Wolf Man* is a better movie than *The Mummy*. I then want to print out copies and put them in personal files to be used to my advantage over the course of the next 20 years." Can we print your opinion about *The Invisible Man* for *our* files?

Gary: Of course you can! Even in the pages of *Midnight Marquee* I have a long history of feeling very lukewarm toward *The Invisible Man*.

Brian: For me, *The Invisible Man* is the perfect Universal horror film. All of the others have some problems, some flaws. A poorly staged scene; a sequence that really doesn't belong; a performance that grates on your teeth. *The Invisible Man* is that rare movie where everything falls into place exactly as it should.

Gary: I almost hate myself for saying this, because no one is a bigger James Whale lover than I am. But, and I confirmed this with a recent viewing, Whale's *Invisible Man* is dull and very outdated.

Just like *Dracula* (1931), the opening sequences with Claude Rains and Una O'Connor, when Jack Griffin stops at the inn, are classic and continue to resonate. But the episodes where the Invisible Man strips and the Keystone Cops react, running around like lunatics, simply do not work.

The film's middle section at the home of Flora Cranley (Gloria Stuart) and her father (Henry Travers), where Rains' Griffin holds them hostage, lacks spark. Even the murder sequence of Kemp (William Harrigan) is over in a split second, with hardly any dramatic buildup. The sequence with the cordon in the snow is again played for laughs and seems, like so many other sequences, just an excuse to demonstrate the special effects. People who criticize movies today for playing up the special effects should look to *The Invisible Man* for the same thing, and those effects feel so dated today (although they were effective in their time).

Think of *The Invisible Man*, and one generally remembers the first 15 or 20 minutes when the mood was ominous and scary... but, when the tone changes to silly humor, the movie never fully recovers.

"A perfect little film that lacks the flaws of other Universal classics"...I think not. If anything, *The Invisible Man* contains more flaws than any other classic Universal horror, other than *Dracula*.

Brian: Well, I know that Cindy would agree with you on this—she hates *The Invisible Man*. It's probably her least favorite of the major Universal horror films.

Cindy: I reacted quite viscerally a few years ago when I watched *The Invisible Man*. I absolutely *hated* the portrayals of

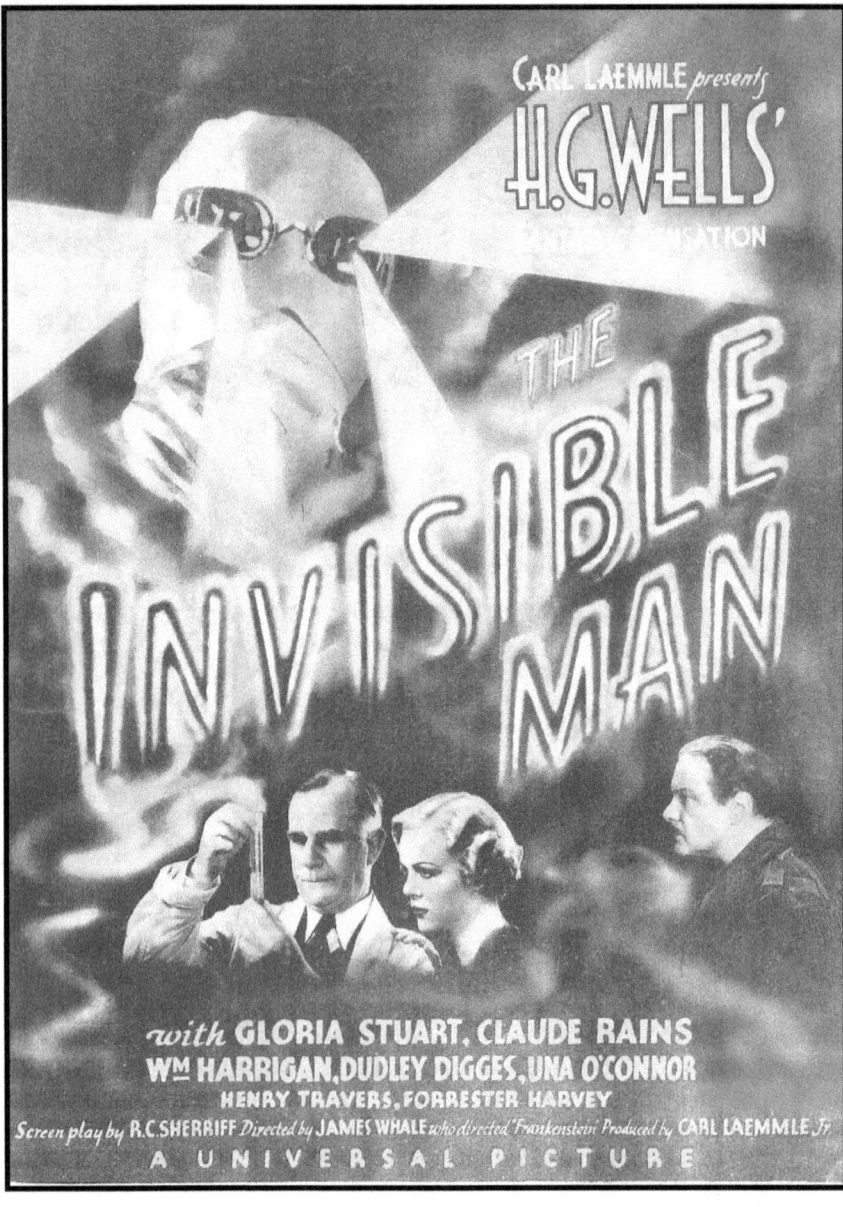

women in the film. And I'm not even an ardent feminist! Gloria Stuart's character needs a few whomps upside the head. And Una O'Connor's comic relief is just insulting. I have never had that sort of reaction to the other Universal movies, even with pale damsels in distress, etc. Just *The Invisible Man*.

I really loathed it.

Arthur: Well, if I hated the female characterizations in *The Invisible Man*, I'd have to hate the female characterizations in virtually every Universal horror film of the 1930s. Instead, I just sigh at what seems to have been a necessary evil and move on.

Cindy: The female characterizations in other Universal movies are nowhere close to the characterizations in this one. My revulsion has nothing to do with the fact that Flora isn't some strong woman reflecting modern/postmodern cinema. As you indicate, the Universal heroines tend not to fit into that category, and I'm fine with that. My revulsion concerns the fact that Flora behaves horribly, and the film gives her a pass just because she's a woman and the psycho is her man—i.e., her behavior is considered "normal female behavior"—and just lets it go at that.

Flora is, in essence, aiding and abetting a psychotic mass murderer...because girls just stand by their man. I don't recall anything comparable in the Universal canon.

Steven: It may be uncomfortable to watch, but there is a real-life corollary for this. True-life criminal lore is filled with the stories of women who stand by their men, even under the most heinous circumstances.

Cindy: She's our *heroine*, not some gangster moll anti-heroine!

Steven: Well, I haven't seen the film in a while, but I'm struggling to recall a scene in which Flora actively assists Jack Griffin. She could insist that he be turned in to the police, I suppose, but, other than that, I can't recall any deeds that truly make her culpable. Is there a scene that I am I forgetting?

Cindy: I haven't seen it in a while, either. I believe that Flora and Jack meet in one scene, and, according to my recollection, after that encounter she fails to tell the police what she knows. That constitutes aiding and abetting. But please understand that my problem with Flora's behavior is not only that she aids and abets a psychotic mass murderer (yes, that *does* happen in real life). My most serious problem is that the *movie* implicitly assumes that it's the proper role of a woman to stand by her man, even in circumstances such as these.

Arthur: You forced me to watch the movie again. In a key scene, Flora's father tells her that he is going alone to see Griffin. He tells her, "You must leave it to me and Kemp. We shall work day and night to undo this terrible experiment." However, Flora refuses to accept a passive role in this drama, saying, "You must let me go to him. I can do far more with Jack than you or Dr. Kemp. I can persuade him to help you. You're powerless unless he does." And, when she meets Griffin, she does everything in her power to appeal to his humanity. Flora does not assist Griffin or enable him. No, she doesn't go to the authorities. She has more faith in her ability to reach his humanity, and the three scientists' ability to cure him if they work together, than in the police's ability to do any good if they drag Griffin away as a madman. There are moments when she comes close to bringing the old Griffin back, only for his chemically induced madness to carry him away. Even then, she doesn't give up, appealing to him: "Oh, come and stay with us. Let's fight this thing out together." I'm sorry you think this is such a cliché, but, while it may not be deep, I'd argue it is a valid characterization.

Cindy: Let it be noted that Jack is already a demonstrable threat to society when Flora makes appeals to his humanity. Her duty is to turn him over to the police or have him dragged away as a madman...not to try to cure him herself. In refusing to go to

Jack Griffin (Claude Rains), ranting about taking over the world, finds girlfriend Flora (Gloria Stuart) listening.

the authorities, she directly aids and abets Jack. As such, she is an accomplice to his murderous mayhem. And the movie never calls her on it.

Arthur: On the other hand, is Flora that much worse than Kemp, the only secondary character who gets as much screen time as she? She certainly shows more courage. The fact is, the film lacks anything resembling a hero, and the only character who comes close is Flora. She at least behaves decently and always tries to appeal to Jack's good side.

And is Una O'Connor's comic relief qualitatively any different from her husband's or the policeman's?

Cindy: Yes, Una O'Connor's comic relief *is* different. If I recall, there is at least one moment where her husband does not appear to be a complete moron. She, on the other hand, is a dimwit suffering from hysteria throughout. And I can't think of anything comparable in the major Universal canon. Maybe in the lesser Universal efforts, but not in the majors.

Una O'Connor's comic relief usually gives the impression that there's a flesh-and-blood (Cockney) human being underneath the antics. Here, she's nothing but a pack of clichés. Not really human at all. Same with Gloria Stuart's Flora. There's nothing there but cliché.

As a woman, I don't find anything to relate to in either of them. That is *never* the case in other Universals. I see human beings beneath the female clichés in other Universals. Not here.

When I was a little girl, female characters like these made me actively wish I didn't have to be part of the same sex as them. I wanted *nothing* to do with them. And I still find them horribly uncomfortable to watch. The other Universal heroines have never had that effect on me. This film is at least borderline misogynistic—and that's a term that I, unlike feminist critics who find misogyny everywhere, don't throw around lightly.

Gary: So, gang, in defending *The Invisible Man* we speak of a screenplay that lacks a discernible hero and features dimly fleshed out characters that never rise above stereotypes? Brian, are you sure this is the perfect Universal horror film model you claim it to be?

Arthur: See, I would argue that virtually all the working-class characters are caricatures—small-minded, petty, self-important. The only difference I can think of offhand is that Una O'Connor is better at making us laugh.

Anthony: When it comes to the humor in *The Invisible Man*, may I suggest that many people find the black comedy/camp/satire of *Bride of Frankenstein* (1935) to be just fine (whereas I

Never has a Universal monster been as diminutive as Claude Rains or featured white as the fiend's dominant color.

think it creates a problem of tone for the film). On the other hand, some people (well, Gary, I guess) feel that the comic portions of *The Invisible Man* do *not* work. May I argue that, on the contrary, they're more in place here than in *Bride*? I hope this doesn't sound too farfetched, but the thing about *The Invisible Man* is that we don't know, necessarily, at the beginning just *what* Jack Griffin is—hero, menace, clown? His gruff, secretive manner suggests one thing. The comic hi-jinx that ensue once he unwraps suggest another. We're constantly kept off balance by him and his manner. It reminds me, in a way, of the beginning of *Goodfellas* (1990), when Joe Pesci's character, Tommy DeVito, is introduced. I knew Pesci, previously, as a comedic actor (I'm thinking of his "Okay, okay, okay" character Leo Getz in *Lethal Weapon 2* [1989]). So, when Ray Liotta's Henry Hill is smiling at him and DeVito is asking, "You think I'm funny?" I didn't really understand the underlying menace that was there—which I *think* was director Martin Scorsese's intention. When DeVito erupts into violence, we're doubly shocked. There's some of this, I think, in Claude Rains' Invisible Man. Sometimes he's funny; sometimes he's threatening. (Of course, he's crazy, after all, so we should expect these manic swings.) I think the most chilling thing for me is when he explains his plans to Kemp: (I paraphrase.) "First we'll start with a few murders—ordinary men, important men—just to show we make no distinction."

Steven: I'll confess that *The Invisible Man* is probably the only Universal monster that actually made me feel uneasy. Vampires, werewolves and the walking dead could safely be relegated to fantasyland, but there was something about that ghostly, invisible apparition of Jack Griffin that seemed unnervingly real.

Gary: The problem I have with the lame humor in *The Invisible Man* is that the film starts off as decidedly horror—a foreboding winter setting, with snow blowing over a drab English village; the heavily bandaged and goggled face of a presumably mutilated stranger (Griffin), whose appearance causes apprehension. His gruff demand for a room and *privacy* is even more off-putting and creepy—we are obviously in Universal horror-mythos territory. But the climax of this beginning third of the story arc involves the "Keystone Cops" running around a room looking, speaking and acting foolishly. And we punctuate that horrible shift in tone with the special-effects display that shouts, "Look at me!" Because this horror story arc climaxes with such silliness, the comic tone seems inappropriate and ruinous. Such a tone undermines the horrific elements contantly.

In contrast, the black humor (never silly) in *Bride of Frankenstein* is the comic relief and sense of wonder leading up to the horrific climax. In fact, one could argue that the black humor is used in *Bride of Frankenstein* as Shakespeare intended, in that we have some tremendous horror sequences (in the bowels of the burned windmill) and need some comic relief before we get into the kidnapping and creation sequences. *Bride* knows just where to put the humor...as a *precursor* to the horrific, *not* as the ultimate climax. The comic tone makes *Bride* brilliant and *Invisible Man* inane. Perhaps *Invisible Man* was a rehearsal for director James Whale to finally get the tone of humor and horror right two years later.

Bryan: Gary, I disagree completely here. The *Invisible Man* scene you cite begins comically enough, with the Invisible One playing harmless pranks on officious policemen and bar patrons (and focusing on the impressive and oh-so-realistic-looking special effects), but it soon escalates into the horror of death itself—as Griffin smashes a copper's face in with a stool, killing him. This mirrors/foreshadows perfectly the plight of the fast-deteriorating pro/antagonist himself, whose mental state is going from light hearted elation to murderous madness. It's a real shocker moment, and one that presages the horrors to come, both the intimate horror of Griffin's plight (separation and alienation from the rest of humanity) and the terrible danger he poses (his increasingly murderous and destructive rampage).

Steven: To me, the humor in *The Invisible Man* serves two functions. First, it is a realistic reaction to a given situation—people often do act foolishly when they are frightened or disoriented. Second, it creates an interesting dynamic between the viewer and the character of Jack Griffin. In the early scenes, we identify with Griffin as he eludes the police, pulls practical jokes on the stupid townsfolk and generally raises harmless hell. Later, of course, we realize that Griffin is spiraling out of control, and we are angry with ourselves for having been duped, or perhaps we have a sense of complicity for vicariously participating in his early displays of dementia.

Does it work? I suppose that depends upon the viewer. But, to me, the humor is more successfully integrated into the plot of *The Invisible Man* than in *Bride*. Despite the overall superiority of the latter film, I always feel a bit uncomfortable with its comic moments, as though they are somewhat jarring to the overall mood of the film. Perhaps my expectations are different—it *is* a Frankenstein film, after all—but I find myself more willing to accept the whimsical actions of the Invisible One and, conversely, wishing that James Whale had toned down the excesses of *Bride*'s secondary characters just a tad. Humor may be more personal than any other emotion. So, if someone doesn't crack a smile when E.E. Clive's policeman whacks at the open air with his nightstick or when Jack Griffin traipses down a country lane chanting, "Here we go gathering nuts in May," I certainly understand. But I think that these are the moments that give *The Invisible Man* a unique feel all its own.

Anthony: I guess it's a matter of perception. Allow me to play the devil's advocate and argue about the humor, as placed, in *Invisible Man* and *Bride*. Gary makes a good point about the horror buildup in *The Invisible Man*'s first third, culminating in the spectacle of the Invisible Man "revealing" himself and the alarmed villagers all aflutter trying to catch him. There is both horror and humor in seeing nothing. And certainly the audience is encouraged to laugh at the antics of the Invisible Man as he puts the people to shame. But that's, I think, to keep the audience off balance. They think of him at this point (because they haven't seen him kill anyone) as a humorous menace. Certainly the

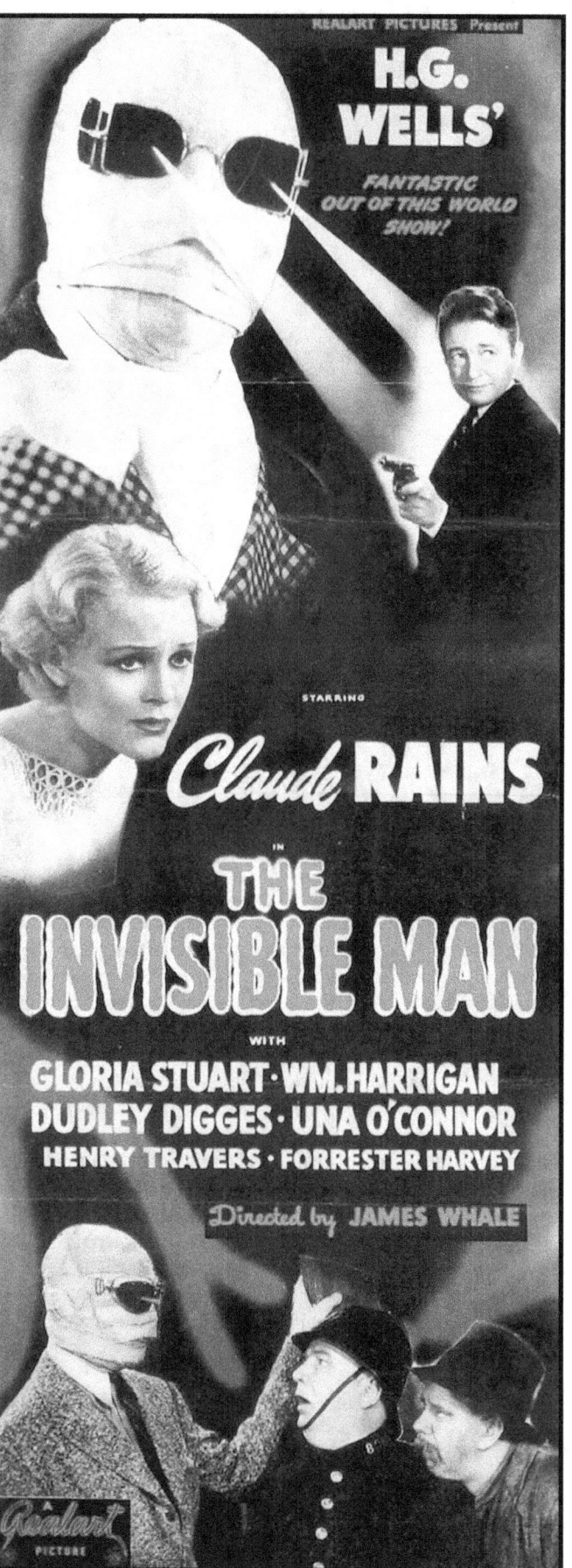

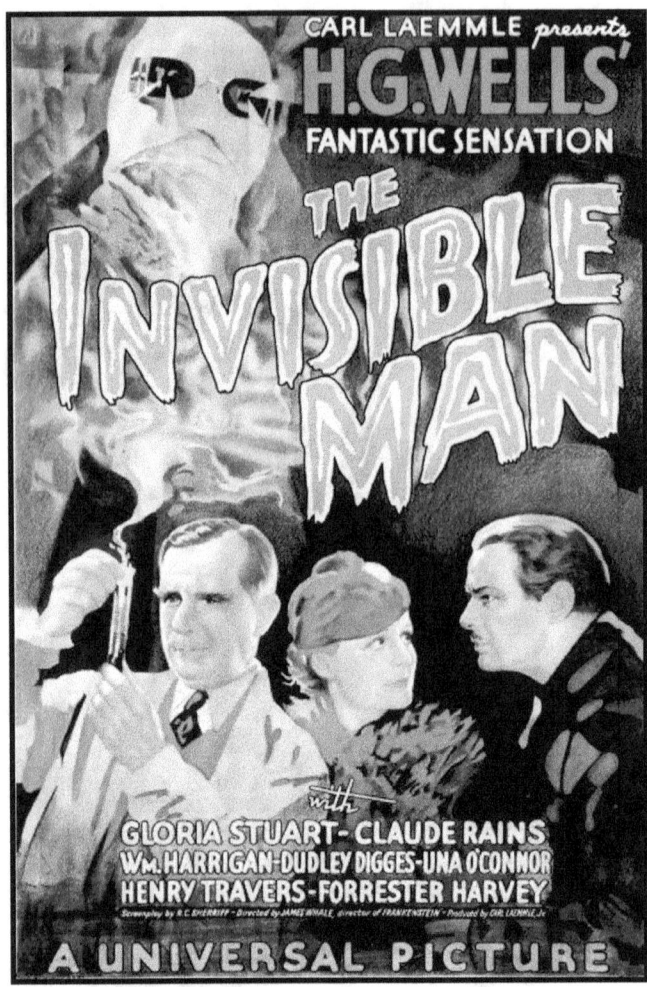

you know it's *the Monster!*" We, the audience, know Karloff's below, but the old woman doesn't suspect a thing. So the horror is that much more intense because we know more than she knows, and we know that hand does not belong to her husband. This is a thrilling sequence, not a comical one.

Admittedly, Minnie the Maid's brief three-four second sequence at the end is played strictly for laughs, with her mugging reactions, audible chirpings and startled turns played to be eccentrically comical.

But, Anthony, don't you see the two sequences are not parallel? And here's why. *The Invisible Man*'s story arc is played with a solemn air of mystery and suspense. The Invisible Man is a monster and a madman. But that first-third story arc culminates with that silly (did someone say *whimsical*?) humorous chase (which could have been out of Abbott and Costello). *Bride of Frankenstein* is totally different. That first sequence is played for its horror impact and ends with the Monster's killing the two elderly people. The Minnie the Maid sequence is a brief coda to the intensity of what the Monster has done. It is classic Shakespearean comic relief (only a few seconds long) that punctuates and relieves the horror sequence that came before. *The Invisible Man* errs by making the too-long Keystone Cop chase sequence the actual climax of the story arc and thus weakens both its horror and dramatic effect. If the entire mayhem-in-the-dark-waters-of-the-mill sequence had been played for humor, the two sequences would have been parallel. But *Bride of Frankenstein* features a horrific sequence with a four-second comic-relief coda that breaks the tension. On the other hand, *The Invisible Man*'s slowly mounted terror is dissipated and ruined by having a comedy sequence as the climax. The brief murder coda in its

hapless people in the inn aren't particularly amused but rather frightened by his behavior. As for *Bride*, we already have the image of the monster from the first film in our minds, so we know what he is capable of doing. When he emerges from the water, burned and scarred, it's frightening. When Hans goes down to make sure the monster's dead, we're filled with the anticipatory thrill of deadly mayhem, and that's what happens. But then the poor mother (Mary Gordon, right?) gives her "husband" a hand and gets drowned for her troubles. That sort of ends the scene on a blackly humorous note, no? Not only that, but then the monster climbs out of the ruined windmill and confronts Una O'Connor's maid, who takes one look at him (or maybe *double*-takes a look at him) and runs screaming into the night. Now, is that comedy, or is that comedy? (Think Abbott and Costello.) In order to suggest that the humor in *Invisible Man* works, I must, of necessity, compare it to *Bride* and run the risk of getting slammed with the title of *Bride* basher once again. Honest, I'm only trying to show the similarities here.

Gary: Look at the sequence in the basement of the windmill. It's played for fright with the growling, shocking appearance of the Monster, resulting in the killing of the old man and old woman. This is iconic Universal horror, with an owl's wink of humor noted briefly. The woman leaning over to lend her husband a hand up is ironic humor at its wittiest, with I bet the entire audience screaming out loud: "Don't give him your hand! Don't

A Belgian poster for *The Invisible Man*

final seconds is too little too late. The use of humor is drastically different. The Keystone Cops chase sequence goes on and on for several minutes, while the Minnie the Maid reaction to Karloff's antics lasts a few seconds.

Bryan: I'm nonplussed to see several of you fine, discerning folks tossing transparent taunts at the Invisible One. I just can't *see* such an *opaque* point of view; obviously you people aren't thinking *clearly* enough. (Heh.)

Okay, I mean, really, is there a more engaging use of the voice in all of Golden Age Horror than Claude Rains' brilliant audio rendition of Griffin? Warm and tender one moment, grandiosely megalomaniacal the next—and with a downright terrifying undercurrent under it all. And the dialogue that he makes his own (everything from "We'll begin with a few murders—murders of great men, murders of little men, just to show we make no distinction" to "Even the moon is frightened of me!") inspires chills. And only perhaps in *The Old Dark House* (1932) does Whale's black humor shine as darkly. The scene of a pair of apparently disembodied trousers skipping down a country lane singing "Here We Go Gathering Nuts in May," sending locals scurrying in terror, is terrifyingly funny. And Una O'Connor's fussy, hysterical barmaid in *The Invisible Man* is much better integrated into the story (and far more amusing) than her screeching harpy version of comic relief that mars *Bride of Frankenstein*. For me, *The Invisible Man* is the full package.

Mark: I agree. I think *Invisible Man* is the Whale film that blends horror and humor most perfectly.

Arthur: And Lundquist makes three.

Gary, it looks like you and I are seeing two completely separate films. You make the opening of *The Invisible Man* sound as humorless as the first 10 minutes of Tod Browning's *Dracula*, followed by an abrupt switch to "Keystone Cops shenanigans." I seemed to remember there being a lot of humor in there. So, to be sure, I went over the film again last night. (Judi's going to hate me for "wasting my time" again. [*Note:* "Judi" is Arthur's significant other, actress Judi Polson, who played Liam Neeson's sister in *Kinsey* (2004).]) This is what I found:

The film begins with Jack Griffin, covered in bandages, walking in the snow. No humor there.

We go to The Lion's Head. *Gag #1*: No sooner are we inside than we see a bar patron interrupting a dart game so a barmaid can walk through in safety. *Gag #2*: Two patrons share a joke about a boy stuck in a snowdrift. *Gag #3*: A man pretends to finger the ivories of what turns out to be a player piano.

Griffin enters, and the humor pauses a moment. *Gag #4*: We are introduced to and contrast the manically energetic Jenny (Una O'Connor) and her assistant, the lethargic and slightly mentally challenged Millie (Merle Tottenham). Jenny leads Griffin up to his room, then returns to get him lunch. *Gag #5*: Actually, this is a series of gags. When Jenny is alone with Griffin, she exhibits elaborate verbal and gestural pretensions of refinement. When she is among her peers, she is suddenly slovenly and slightly drunk. When running back and forth between the two worlds, she chatters under her breath like Popeye in a Max Fleischer cartoon. Her changing behavior becomes even funnier every time she shares space with the lugubrious Millie. This sort of humor fills up the running time until the film's first shock shot, her first sight of Griffin's invisible face, to which (*Gag #6*) she reacts.

There follows a comical exchange between Jennie and the bar patrons until the scene changes to the home of Doctor and Flora Cranley, and for a while there is no humor at all.

All this humor is completely integrated into the action of the film. And it is not slapstick humor; it is character humor, rooted in British Music Hall, which lets us get to know the community that will soon be terrorized by the Invisible Man.

Gary: And…such "gags" are supposed to strengthen your claim that the initial sequences with Rains are not horrifically toned but comically toned (or at least a blending of the two)? I would counter that even within the first 15 minutes of *Dracula* that the somber tone is punctuated with humorous gags ("I never drink…wine" is just one; some wide-eyed reactions by Dwight Frye are played for laughs; some of Bela Lugosi's body language elicits smiles; etc.) that do not dilute the intensely dank tone. Your quasi-comical barroom banter only emphasizes the horror when the bandaged Invisible Man enters the tavern and stops such banter dead in its tracks. Even the most intense Universal horror sequences almost always have comical banter or visual winks (such as the owl sequence to punctuate the killings at the start of *Bride of Frankenstein*), and such tidbits do not dominate the tone but serve as a contrast to emphasize the horrific tone.

Mark: I'll say it again: *The Invisible Man* is Whale's most seamless blend of horror and humor. Thanks, Arthur, for breaking down the opening scene to demonstrate, specifically, how this integration is accomplished.

Gary: But such blending of humor and horror can be found not only in *The Invisible Man* and *Dracula*, but also in *The*

Una O'Connor and the mysterious snow-covered stranger create the aura of horror initially, but as the film progresses, the horror becomes diluted, so says Gary.

Black Cat (1934), *Bride of Frankenstein*, *The Old Dark House* and *Dracula's Daughter* (1936). Your claim of "most seamless blend" is the only debatable point here.

Arthur: The humor in the beginning of *The Invisible Man* is not qualitatively different from the humor we see in what Gary calls the "Keystone Cops" sequence later (where, by the way, there is only one cop present), where the biggest laughs come from character lines like "Look! 'E's all eaten away!" and "'Ow can I handcuff a bloomin' shirt?" We have already been prepared for the humor in the latter scene by what we have previously seen in the film's opening.

Gary: True, only one cop is present in my so-called "Keystone Cops" sequence, but that one officer is joined by three bar patrons who, joining in with the cop, run around like idiotic fools in a sight gag culminating when the officer hits one of the innocent bar patrons over the head with his Billy club, missing the Invisible One by miles. Such silly shenanigans are directly inspired from the Keystone Cops-style of slapstick humor.

Anthony: Those of you who like the movie more than Gary, is there anything that mars it for you? Would those of you who rate the movie highly agree that it is the best treatment of invisibility in the movies?

Steven: The climax of *The Invisible Man* doesn't quite have the punch of the decade's best horror films. Once Griffin's menace becomes widely publicized, the film becomes more of a chase and adventure story and loses the emphasis on horror that made the initial reels so memorable. But, other than that, I find the film to be quite solid. And, no, I cannot think of another movie about invisibility that handles the dramatic possibilities of this topic nearly as well.

Anthony: Agreed.

Gary: Well put, Steven. What begins as a classic Universal horror picture quickly becomes a special-effects laden horror-comedy and ultimately forgets about its horrifying beginning to become a "chase and adventure" film. My, the film appears to be neither fish nor fowl and seems to jump all over the map, never setting upon one definable tone or able to make up its mind... is it horror, comedy, adventure or simply Universal mishmash?!!!

Anthony: There is both humor and horror in seeing nothing. That's why invisibility is a "touchy" subject for a movie, because it can so easily be played for laughs. And has. The *Topper* films (*Topper* [1937], *Topper Returns* [1939], and *Topper Takes a Trip* [1941]), although they're about ghosts, use invisibility tricks for comedy. So does 1941's *The Invisible Woman*. As for *Abbott and Costello Meet the Invisible Man* (1951), Jeff Miller has some interesting things to say about it in Midnight Marquee Press' *You're Next! Loss of Identity in the Horror Film*; he considers the film a sort of remake of *The Invisible Man Returns* (1940) and suggests that the madness angle kind of jars with Abbott and Costello's comedy.

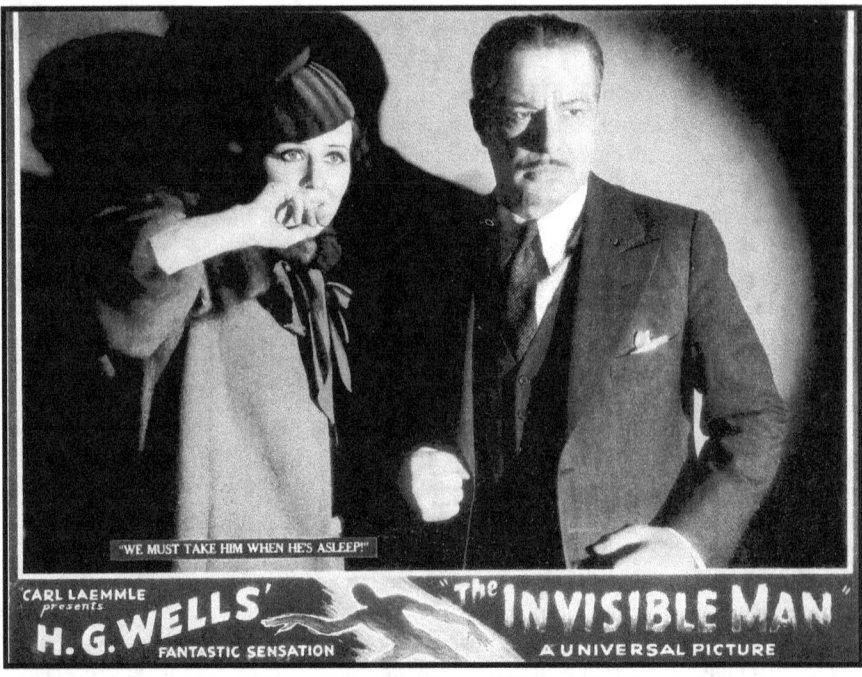

Fearful, Flora (Gloria Stuart) and Dr. Kemp (William Harrigan) fight onward.

Several raunchy 1980s comedies (e.g., *The Invisible Kid* [1988]) use invisibility as an opportunity for a guy to spy, unobserved, on naked women. *Invisible Man Returns* plays it straight, doesn't it? Although, like *Invisible Agent* (1942), I'm not sure it stresses the horror angle so much. In *Returns*, invisibility is a gimmick the hero can use to prove his innocence (while racing against time, before the drug drives him insane); In *Agent*, it's used as a tool against the Axis (I believe there's a fear the hero might go mad if he stays invisible too long). *Invisible Man's Revenge* (1944) alternates gruesomeness with some comedy involving Leon Errol as the invisible man's sidekick, and Paul Verhoeven tried, in *The Hollow Man* (2000) with Kevin Bacon, to make his invisible man a pretty disgusting sexual assailant, if I'm remembering correctly. And invisibility *can* be pretty horrifying. Isn't that the terror inherent in Ambrose Bierce's "The Damned Thing"?

Gary: "There is both humor and horror in seeing nothing. That's a great line, Anthony. But, as that line applies to *The Invisible Man*, simply too much humor underlies its horror tone. My problem with *The Invisible Man* is that I can't get past those silly Keystone Cop shenanigans with the strip-teasing invisible man running around the room in his white shirt. The movie begins darkly with Jack Griffin, resembling a mutilated human wreck, renting—with apparently sinister intentions—a private back room. But this horrific beginning leads to the Keystone Cops chase with its very traditional slapstick, physical humor. Even if, as Bryan notes, such silliness ends with the death of a cop, too much time has been wasted on gleeful exhilaration for us to be reminded that, oh yeah, this is meant to be frightening. The balance is off; the tone is askew.

James Whale matured greatly as a director and a manipulator of cinematic tone two years later in 1935 when he made *Bride of Frankenstein*.

Anthony: For me, he was already a mature director when he made his incontrovertible masterpiece, *Frankenstein* (1931), two years before *The Invisible Man*. Once he'd satisfied the studio by giving it the horror thriller it wanted, he was free to do whatever *he* wanted in the genre: hence, *The Invisible Man*, *Old Dark House* and *Bride*.

Arthur: Indeed, one might say that James Whale matured greatly as a director between *Hell's Angels* (1930) and *Frankenstein*, were it not for the fact that Whale's work in *Hell's Angels* is pretty damn good. [*Note:* Whale is credited as dialogue director on *Hell's Angels*, but he actually wrote and directed much of the film officially credited to producer Howard Hughes.]

Gary: I think the bottom line is this: People who enjoy *The Invisible Man* the most chuckle at its traditional slapstick humor, while those who enjoy *Bride of Frankenstein* the most appreciate its eccentric black humor. *Bride of Frankenstein*'s quirky humor is dark and morbid (Thesiger's picnic in the crypt, the strange miniature people, the sequence with the Blind Hermit and the Monster with its classic "Smoke…good!" and all the bits with

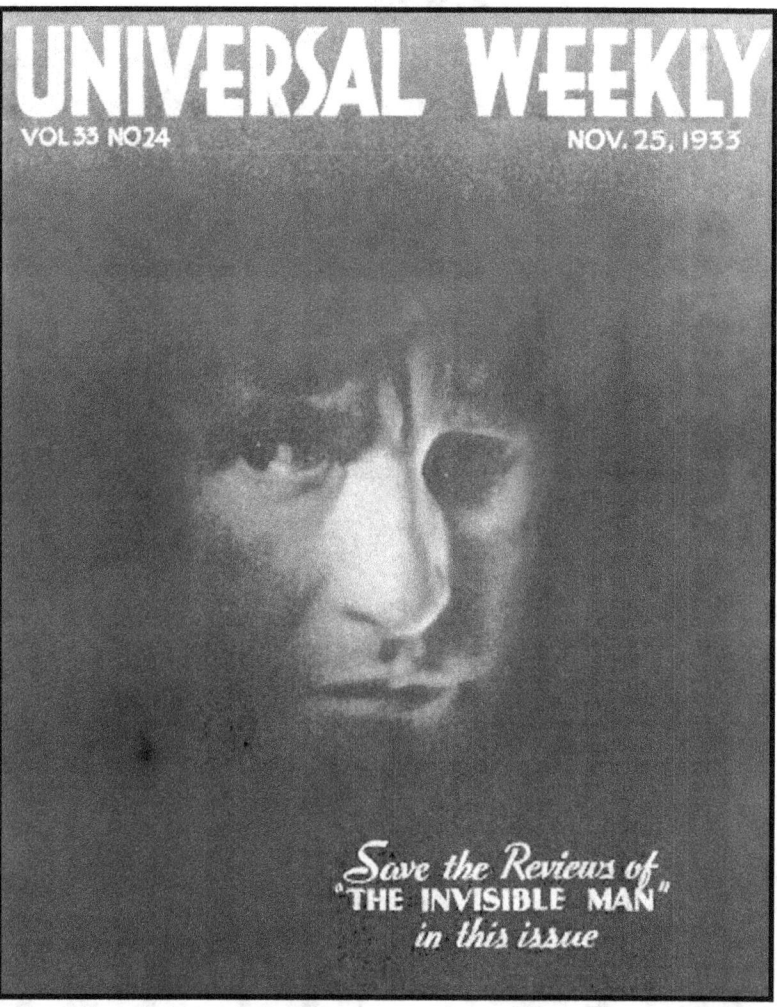

Minnie) while the humor of *The Invisible Man* is mostly silly. Some people are turned off by *Bride*'s off-putting humor, while those of us who go wild for *Bride* find the humor of *The Invisible Man* puts them off.

Steven: My feeling is that James Whale had different goals for each film. In *The Invisible Man*, Whale picked up on the black humor of *The Old Dark House* and pushed it to the limit. As a result, the film is played as much for laughs as it is for chills. In *Bride*, Whale wasn't aiming for obvious comedy—instead he was crafting a dry send-up of the genre. The horror is established early on, but Whale slyly shifts gears and plays much of the film in satiric mode. Both films are subtle enough that they can be read as straight thrillers, but, to their credit, each one works on a secondary level as well.

It's interesting, in fact, that Whale's shockers all vary so widely in tone. One (*Frankenstein*) is a straight-ahead horror tale, one (*The Old Dark House*) is a macabre comedy of manners, one (*The Invisible Man*) is a black comedy, and one (*Bride of Frankenstein*) is a subtle horror satire. Even when crafting something as obvious as a sequel, Whale had the innate good taste to stretch and explore a new direction. I only wish that more directors who dabbled in horror films had such acute sensibilities.

Gary: Steven, your final point is indeed a good one, and a very nice way to end our discussion!

A Lot of Bug On A Little Budget

by Doug Lamoreux

It's no fun watching a movie with me. I'm a writer and actor, which means I dissect every picture I see microscopically and render immediate adoration and/or criticism. God help you if I'm holding the remote. As a passionate filmmaker, I'm completely unimpressed with massive production budgets. I'd rather watch Roger Corman's *It Conquered the World* than Peter Jackson's *King Kong* any day of the week. If anyone wants a "thumbs up" from me, he/she will need to put some effort into it.

Which brings me to *The Deadly Mantis,* a 1957 Universal-International release unjustly treated by critics and film historians alike for 50 years. It was rarely seen or mentioned until its recent DVD release. Modern (read that "young") critics, for whom the Cold War is something fought with NyQuil, are unable to relate to its social tenor, to understand the politics of its day, to forgive its low budget or to enjoy the gem-like moments of entertainment *The Deadly Mantis* offers.

The story proper opens with an extended documentary (narrated by Marvin Miller, the baritone voice of Robby the Robot in *Forbidden Planet*) highlighting the construction of the radar "fences" that protect our nation's coastlines and, more pointedly, our continental northern borders. This sequence is far from superfluous, as some suggest, or included to add running time to a short script, but its inclusion is vital to the plot and necessary for an understanding of the era in which the mantis makes his appearance.

Genuine fears existed for "our" need to prepare for an attack from "them." The fact that the potential enemy remained unnamed, in our film and in daily life, made it even more frightening. As Frances Bavier so accurately says in *The Day the Earth Stood Still*, "And you know whom I mean." Was it paranoia? Certainly. The writer of *The Deadly Mantis*, Martin Berkeley (who also penned the screenplays for *Tarantula, Revenge of the Creature* and wrote additional dialogue for Vincent Price's 1946 film *Shock*), would wind up being famous as a "namer" for Sen. Joseph McCarthy's notorious House Un-American Activities Committee. Berkeley's testimony damaged and in some cases ended the careers of dozens in Hollywood. Was it all paranoia? The Cuban Missile Crisis suggests otherwise. Suffice to say, the 1950s and 1960s were a turbulent and sometimes terrifying time in our history. The Cold War was real. The fears played upon by *The Deadly Mantis* were real, as well.

The documentary concludes with the completion of the DEW line [the Distant Early Warning radar line established just below the North Pole] and the arrival of Colonel Joe Parkman (Craig Stevens) to command Red Eagle One, the nerve center of the supersonic radar shield.

Stevens, we may remember, first came to genre notice in *Abbott & Costello Meet Dr. Jekyll and Mr. Hyde*, putting the moves on Karloff's niece. He's best remembered as the Bond-like Peter Gunn in the television series of the same name, that ran from 1958-61. He later had recurring roles on *Dallas* and *The Invisible Man* series with David McCallum. Stevens returned briefly to the world of nasty bugs for Curtis Harrington's made-for-TV movie, *Killer Bees*.

Barely has Parkman's chair warmed when disasters begin to strike. A DEW line weather station is destroyed. The Red Eagle One pilots are scrambled to chase a radar blip that vanishes as quickly as it appeared. A C47 is knocked from the sky. Parkman investigates the devastated scenes. Both the radar station and the plane are crushed, the men are missing and there are no bodies. At each scene, a strange set of skid marks, eight-and-a-half-feet wide, have been left in the snow, as if something came in for a landing. And lodged in the fuselage of the plane is a five-foot-long organic "spur" that gives every indication of having been torn from some living creature.

When the military, represented by General Ford (Donald Randolph), and science, represented by Professor Gunther (Florenz Ames), are unable to identify the origin of the spur, they call in Dr. Nedrick Jackson (William Hopper), Chief Paleontologist of Washington, D.C.'s Museum of Natural History.

Randolph appeared mostly in Westerns and on TV, but worked with Vincent Price in *The Mad Magician*. Ames was 74 years old when he appeared in *The Deadly Mantis* and seemed every bit the wise, no-nonsense professor. Nothing could have been further from the truth. Ames and his wife Alice "Adelaide" Winthrop were singing and dancing veterans of 40 years on the vaudeville circuit. Ames had also done an off-and-on stint from 1950-54 playing Inspector Richard Queen on television's *The Adventures of Ellery Queen*.

Colonel Joe Parkman (Craig Stevens) compares a picture of an actual mantis with a model plane to show the relative size of the gigantic insect.

Hopper, the son of *Dracula's Daughter* alum Hedda Hopper, made his first sojourn to the world of horror in *The Return of Doctor X,* billed by his actual first name DeWolf. His other genre appearances include *Conquest of Space, The Bad Seed* and the lead in Ray Harryhausen's *20,000,000 Miles To Earth*. Television soon snatched Hopper up and from 1957-66 he played P.I. Paul Drake in 162 episodes of *Perry Mason*.

An examination of the spur and a test of its blood, showing it has no red corpuscles, leads Ned to conclude the spur is from a huge, flesh-eating insect. But what kind of insect? Ned tells us, describing the perfect movie monster:

"I've narrowed the field to one. Now the hook they found on the plane may very well be a spur from its foreleg. If this is it, as large as the monstrous creature we're looking for, I doubt whether anything that ever lived could be as deadly. It's strong beyond anything its size suggests. It walks, leaps and flies. Its appetite is insatiable. In all the kingdom of the living, there is no more deadly or voracious creature than the praying mantis."

Huge, flesh-eating, insatiable… Yeah, babe, this is my kind of monster. Better than that, like the very best of the cinema's city stomping creatures, he's completely destructive without being malevolent. In Ned's words: "I'm convinced that we're dealing with a mantis in whose geological world the smallest insects were as large as man, and now failing to find those insects as food, well… it's doing the best that it can."

Let me pause to insist that arguments that *The Deadly Mantis*' "science" is laughable are…laughable. It's a movie about a huge bug on a rampage. I confess no evidence exists in the fossil record suggesting a giant praying mantis ever existed. Neither is there any record of Godzilla, Rodan, shrews the size of retrievers, giant Gila Monsters, huge ants (in or outside of their empires), VW-sized rats, Jeep-sized Razorbacks, turkey buzzards with giant claws or massive mollusks challenging any part of the world. We've entered a land of make believe where normally small and inoffensive creepy crawlers suddenly loom large and, hopefully, terrifying to the human psyche. The wonderful fantasy world of "What if…," if anyone wants real science, watch *Nova*. If not, sit down and buckle up. Some of us want to ride.

Dr. Jackson's passionate argument that the mantis was frozen alive for millions of years may be hogwash. So what? For once, it's refreshing the menace wasn't brought about because man dabbled in things he was meant to leave alone, because of nuclear fallout or because the Military-Industrial Complex won't stop conspiring. Here, the monster is gargantuan by nature, encased in ice by nature and unleashed by nature. Let the battle begin.

Ned and Marge Blain (Alix Talton), editor of the museum's magazine, visit the DEW line to investigate, but the mantis is on the move. The Mid-Canada radar fence reports a blip moving over 200 mph. Soon, Pine Tree (on the U.S./Canadian border) picks up the UFO as well. Ned determines the creature is headed for the Gulf Stream and then South America, feeding as it travels.

Producer William Alland is a horror film legend. He received his start as an actor with Orson Welles' Mercury Theatre and was a cast member of the infamous 1938 *War of the Worlds* Halloween radio broadcast. He played Thompson, the reporter, in the 1941 classic *Citizen Kane*. In 1952, Alland became a film producer and began making classics of his own, among them *It Came From Outer Space, This Island Earth, Tarantula, The*

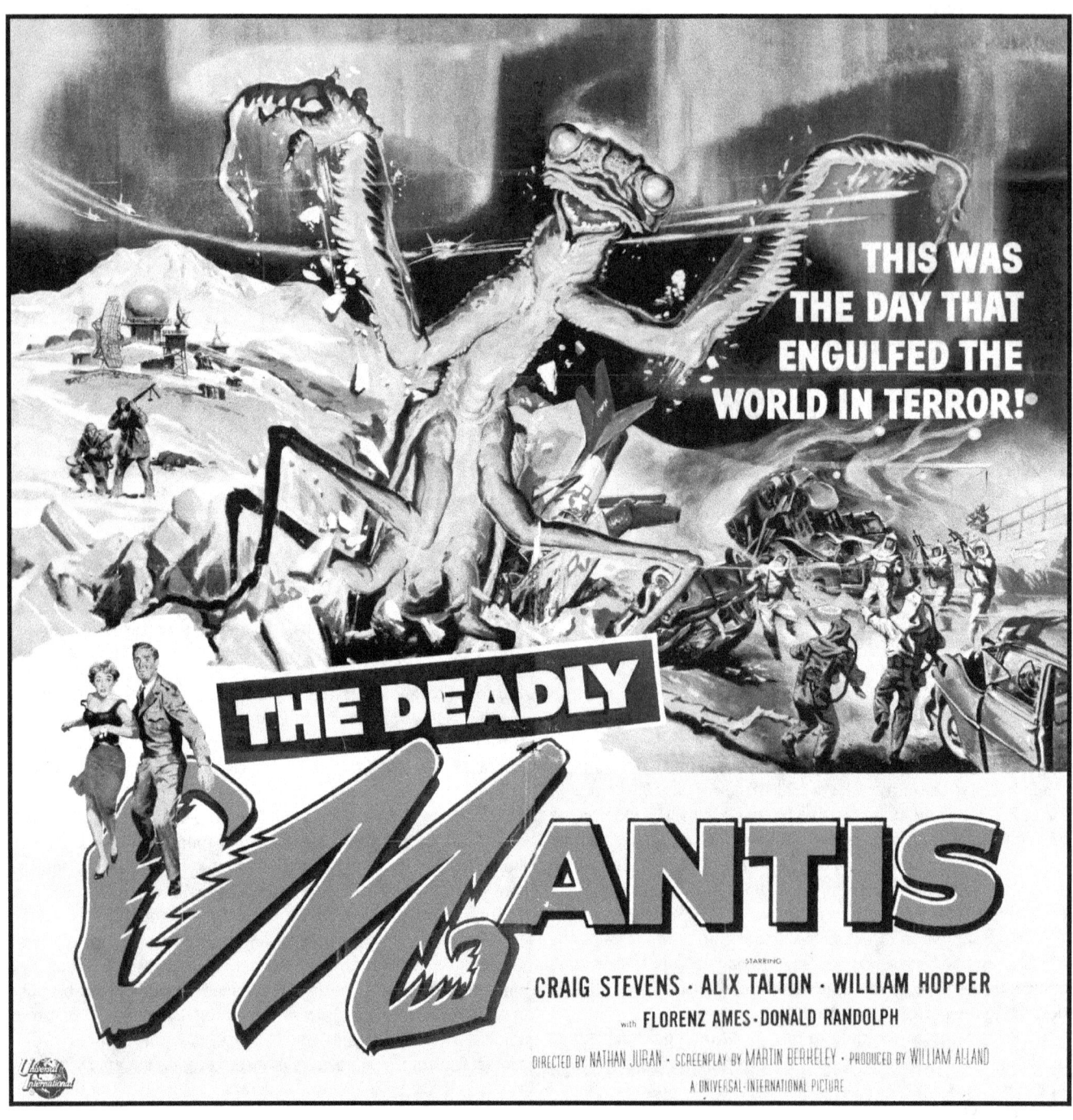

Mole People, The Land Unknown, Colossus of New York, and of course, Creature From The Black Lagoon film series. Nathan Juran directed Alland's first production, Boris Karloff's The Black Castle, in 1952. When The Deadly Mantis came up on his production schedule, Alland sought Juran once more.

One look at Juran's resume makes it clear that when he's good, he's very good; and when he's bad, he's still pretty good. As an art director, Juran gave us The Loves of Edgar Allan Poe, Dr. Renault's Secret and won the 1943 Academy Award for How Green Was My Valley. As a writer, he penned the awful but wacky Doctor Blood's Coffin (as Jerry Juran). He made up for that with the delightful children's fantasy Jack the Giant Killer. Horror and fantasy fans have every reason to respect his directing work, as he gave us the aforementioned The Black Castle and Jack the Giant Killer. He also helmed three Harryhausen classics, 20,000,000 Miles to Earth, The 7th Voyage of Sinbad and First Men in the Moon. He was an Irwin Allen favorite, directing many TV episodes of Voyage to the Bottom of the Sea, Lost in Space, The Time Tunnel and Land of the Giants. Even his bottom of the barrel flicks, Attack of the 50 Foot Woman and Brain From Planet Arous (Nathan Hertz subbing for Juran in Brain from Planet Arous), deliver more bizarre entertainment value than they have any right.

With the fad still raging, and on the heels of their own successful Tarantula, Universal wanted another contender for the "big bug" box-office dollars. But they wanted it done cheaply.

Economy was the name of the game during *The Deadly Mantis'* production. Instrumental in helping Juran accomplish this were Universal's supervising art director Alexander Golitzen and art director Robert Clatworthy. Golitzen would garner 14 Academy Award nominations and three wins during his career, including his first Oscar for work on *Phantom of the Opera* in 1943. Clatworthy would win one Academy Award and earn five nominations, including a nomination for *Psycho* in 1960. Their work is amazing in *The Deadly Mantis*; sets were designed to get the most bang for the buck and redressed creatively for varied uses.

The Arctic base set is, quite frankly, a marvel of good looks and economy; a hall, an office, a radio room and a recreation room all connected by walls that are predominantly windows. No matter which room Juran shot in, business is always going on in the background. The wall separating Parkman's office from the radio room is one huge glass map, inexpensive, but genuinely visual. The radio room was redressed twice. To become the Mid-Canada Operation Center, set decorators Russell A. Causman (who'd been doing his thing at Universal since the 1930s) and Oliver Emert slightly altered the face of the background machinery and crowded Juran's already tight shot with a large map of Canada. To create the armory, they rearranged the desks and brought in a gun rack, while Juran shot the scene from above, eliminating the telltale walls.

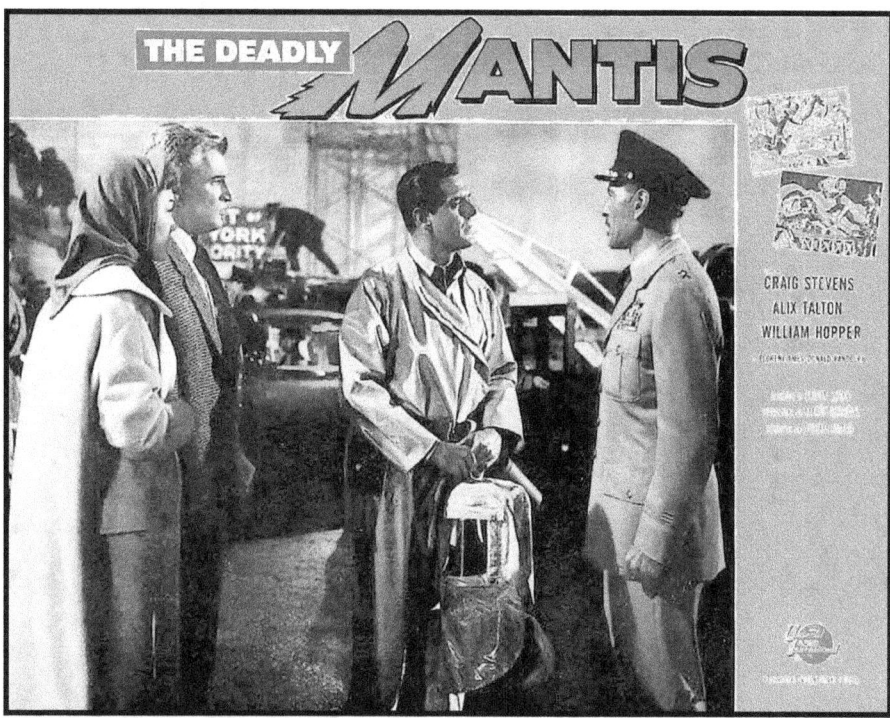
Magazine editor Marge Blain (Alix Talton) and "bug" expert Dr. Jackson (William Hopper) listen in as Parkman talks to the military brass.

Parkman's arrival, the crashed Weather 4 station and the site of the downed C-47 all take place on the same redressed snow-bound set. A gorgeous cyclorama backdrop and a single-prop plane repositioned through these shots add considerable depth to the composition.

Quite practically, if a little bit illogically, the scientific examinations of the spur, the press conferences, the television broadcast, Operation Marge and the radio command sequences for the final air battle all take place in the conference room set outside of General Ford's office.

Not only did they have to redress sets, but they also had to match material from the many stock footage clips that were employed. The term stock footage, particularly in reference to 1950's horror and science fiction films, has been used with the same tone and respect as the phrase leper colony. Such negative judgment is entirely unfair and demonstrates an ignorant position. The list of films that never could have been made without stock footage is endless. The question should be how well the

Dr. Jackson and team look for signs of what exactly attacked the snowbound military compound by checking the debris.

footage helps tell the story; does it blend in to aid the narrative, or does it, unduly, call attention to itself.

An almost unbelievable 12 minutes of *The Deadly Mantis*' 79-minute running time is comprised of stock footage. In the passionate but completely talentless hands of someone like Ed Wood, we might wind up with a hopeless mess like *Plan 9 from Outer Space*. In the talented hands of Juran, we get something altogether different, a documentary-style immediacy. The viewer is not offered haphazard shots of varied aircraft racing across the screen in opposing directions, with the occasional intrusion of an atomic blast, an octopus or an unexplained herd of stampeding buffalo, as occur in many low-budget efforts. Here, Juran gives us entire sequences, pilots scrambling for their machines, readying for their mission, taking-off (including cockpit interiors from the pilot's point of view) and racing as a unit toward the airborne menace. All in a documentary style that heightens the reality of the moment.

True, the aircraft carrier footage employed here is actually of three different ships. The first clip is of the CV-36 USS *Antietam*, the second of the CV-34 USS *Oriskany* and the take-off clips feature the CV-47 USS *Philippine Sea*. But this is splitting hairs with a pretty thin knife. I've visited aboard the USS *John F. Kennedy* and, regardless of one's personal opinions about the military, it cannot be debated these are awe-inspiring vessels. The carrier sequences in the film bring the message home; the battle is on.

Admittedly, when the mantis attacks the Eskimo village, the footage is at first jarring. Were it not for the droning buzz already established to be the creature in flight, we might wonder if we have slipped into a different film. Well, yes. The sequence is taken in total from writer/director Arnold Fanck's German/Danish/American co-production *S.O.S. Eisberg* (1933), starring the infamous documentary filmmaker and actress Leni Riefenstahl. As intrusive as the footage seems, however, Juran yanks the viewer back into his film with a well conceived tag. Utilizing two actors, set pieces and props matching the stock shots and alternating points of view, a believable assault on an Eskimo village is pulled off. Here too, we hear for the first time the "roar" of the mantis, a guttural scream from Hell. This roar, incidentally, would become a television staple in the 1960s when it became the bark of Spot, the pet dragon living under the staircase, in *The Munsters* series. Ultimately, the sequence adds not only a compelling and believable attack scene, but also an overall scope to the film.

The Deadly Mantis features some nice touches not normally seen in a low-budget feature. Juran doesn't just cut in stock

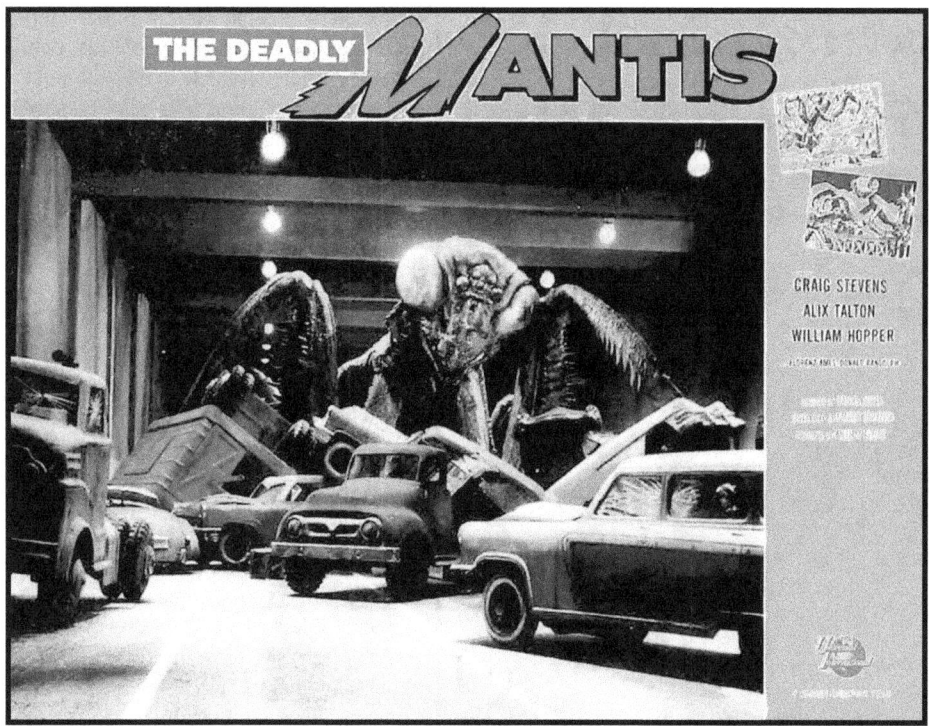

The monstrous mantis, trapped inside the underground traffic tunnel, is the type of classic climax that fans expect.

footage; he dissolves in and out of it. He alters it. He adapts his film around it. The time and attention paid to the lighting by cinematographer Ellis W. Carter deserves special mention.

Carter photographed one of my favorite serials, *King of the Rocket Men*, in 1949 and shot another closet favorite, the vampire-Western *Curse of the Undead* in 1959. In between, he lensed four pictures for Alland.

In *The Deadly Mantis*, the actors' shadows are all over the place…on purpose. Carter always both recognizes and compensates ingeniously for the differences between documentary realism and soundstage realism. With so much stock footage on display, before and after each of the studio produced segments, standard Hollywood lighting would have been unbearably jarring. Carter adjusted, throwing stark shadows against set walls to match the intrusive but real shadows seen in life. This took courage on Carter's part because it eliminated the usual slick look that many confuse with quality. But, when the picture cuts back-and-forth between the press briefing (studio) and the observers at home and at their posts (stock), the transitions are easily accepted as belonging to one reality.

This same sequence is a great example of another technique Juran uses to confuse our senses and draw us into his film. Juran cuts from the press briefing to a family listening to the briefing on a radio. This is a stock shot, but it's taken from a studio-produced film. He then cuts immediately to a family watching the briefing on television. This is a stock shot, filmed on location, but taken from a documentary. But Juran goes to the trouble to matte footage of the press briefing onto the screen of the family watching the television. With Stevens' voice running through the entire sequence and his image appearing in the stock shot, we're again led to accept the reality of the moment. It's a low-budget version of an Alfred Hitchcock technique.

Hitchcock went on location to shoot the sea gulls' attack on Tippi Hedren for *The Birds*. Rod Taylor lifts Hedren from the boat, helps her past the boat house and to the restaurant. Instead of just using the sequence as shot, Hitchcock plays with our realities. He shot a moving plate of the boathouse, put Taylor and Hedren on a treadmill in the studio and rear-projected the boathouse footage behind them, while they walked in place. He cut this into the location footage. Hitchcock determines what is real for the audience. Juran may not be Hitchcock, but I can't help but respect his inexpensive attempt to create realism in *The Deadly Mantis*.

While Universal was home to horror films, it should be remembered they were always the low-rent district as far as the

The military, armed and ready, pursues the deadly mantis in the underground tunnel.

Midnight Marquee #77

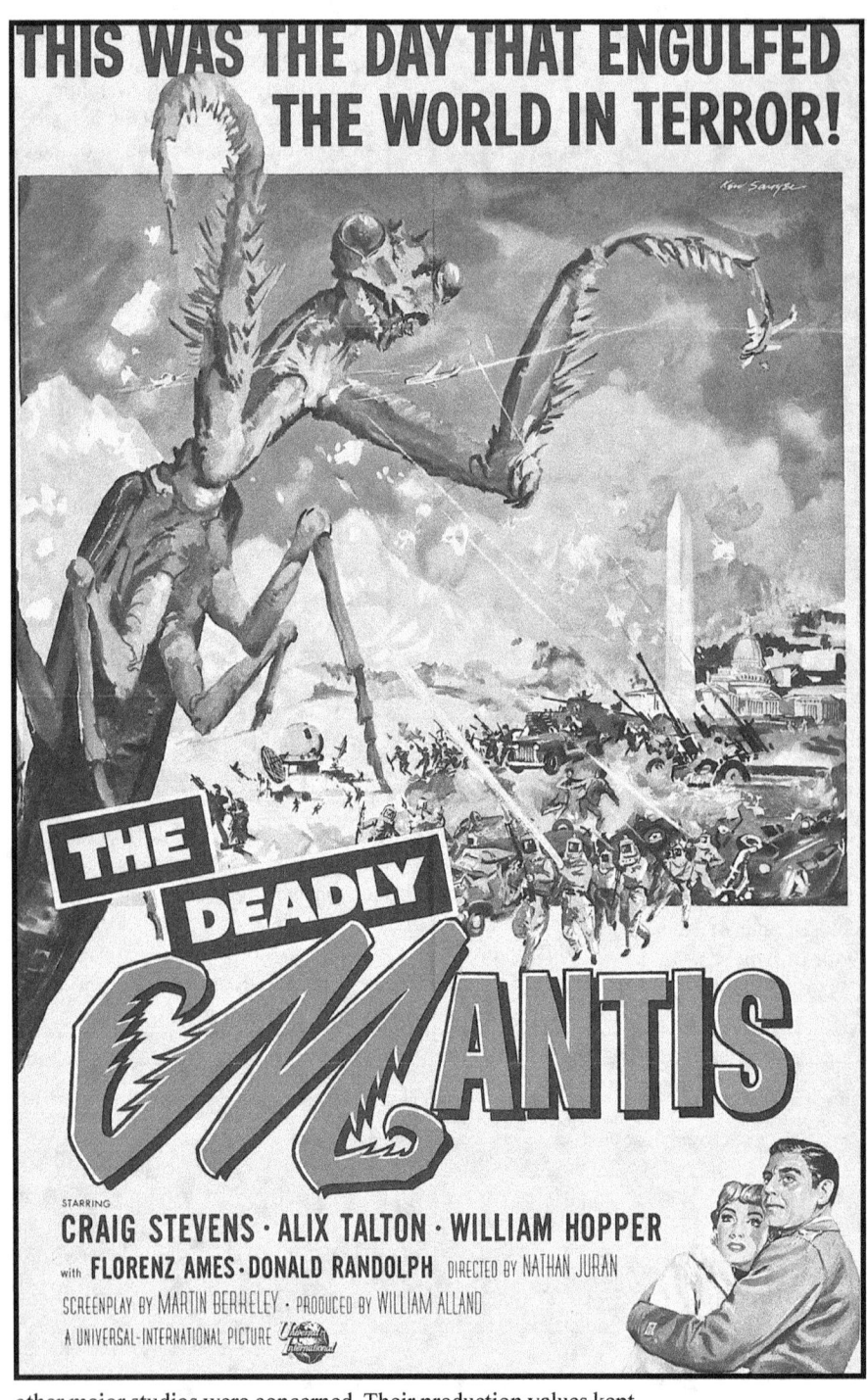

other major studios were concerned. Their production values kept them off skid row, where Monogram, PRC and others operated, but they were not nearly on a par with the likes of MGM or Warner Bros. The point is, Universal got good at making a lot out of very little, including conjuring up inexpensive, but impressive, special effects. *The Dead Mantis* is a prime example.

The sequence of the mantis stalking, then attacking, the Red Eagle One Arctic base is beautifully realized and effectively believable. The mantis, a nifty stick puppet operated from below and behind, marches across the tabletop landscape with real menace and, eventually, begins tearing the building apart. On Universal's process stage, the monster's massive head is rear projected behind the window of the interior set. The actors run in panic as debris drops on them. (Quick eyes will note a small piece of ceiling falls behind Hopper *before* the mantis strikes.) Watch how the instant the actors clear the frame, the action accelerates. The film was processed optically (frames skipped in printing) to speed up the visuals and elevate the apparent violence of the destruction. That attention to detail earns my respect.

The action switches outside for one of the film's most thrilling moments, when the men take a flamethrower to the monster in a snowstorm. It's a standard "big bug" moment, but carried off with a lot of care, becoming quite believable.

Note the stark set-up employed by Juran, editor Chester Schaeffer and Clifford Stine's special-effects team in a late scramble scene at Andrews Air Force Base: A tight shot of a pilot in his cockpit (stock), another pilot in his cockpit (stock), Stevens in a cockpit mock-up on the Process Stage (studio) and a plane taking off (stock)—all blended seamlessly.

During one of the film's late air battles, process photographer Tom McCrory even gives us a shot of the mantis as seen from the pilot's point of view, inside the cockpit of a pursuing jet. It's a rare extra mile to have gone for a low-budget film.

The matte work employed during the mantis flyovers of Washington and those used for the creature's final plunge into Manhattan are also a cut above the usual low budget fare. Stine, who got his start in the business as a second assistant camera operator on the original *King Kong*, shows why he was the man to succeed the legendary John P. Fulton as Universal's effects wizard.

Likewise, the monster's assault on the Washington Monument is a visually captivating moment. In a terrific composite, a live praying mantis is printed optically climbing a photograph of the monument. Stine then cuts to the very top of the structure, the only portion actually constructed in miniature, and back to the mantis puppet which clings to it as the scene ends, with its forelegs being manipulated from above like a marionette. Here, I have to admit, some frustration creeps in. We big-bug maniacs came for destruction and the production couldn't afford to deliver a payoff. Neatly composed, the scene leaves the viewer hungry for more.

Bad weather is good for monsters. A disappointed Walt Disney scrubbed the original giant squid battle sequence in *20,000 Leagues Under the Sea* because it took place backed by a gorgeous orange sunset. The same sequence was re-shot during a raging thunderstorm on a churning sea and became a classic moment in cinema. Rain, darkness, snow and fog heighten the suspense—and hide the wires.

It's not surprising that when Mrs. Farley (Helen Jay) gets off a city bus in a heavy fog bad things happen. No sooner does the bus pull away then it is grabbed by the mantis, lifted off the ground and slammed down on its side. Jay's blood-curdling scream almost makes up for her stilted line readings a moment earlier. She made a surprising number of appearances in genre films, nearly all of them in small, uncredited roles, including *Space Master X-7*, *The Space Children*, *I Married A Monster from Outer Space* and *Simon, King of the Witches*.

Like all of the attack sequences in the film, the bus scene is short but sweet. The bus and mantis shots were creatively manipulated for a well-balanced scene. In a scene that helps drive the story, the fog adds both claustrophobia and scope at the same time.

The finale also takes place in fog. The wounded mantis ditches into the Manhattan Tunnel. The military has thrown tarps over both ends of the tunnel and filled it with smoke, hoping to disorient the creature and provide cover for a ground assault team, while the fire department wets the tarps to seal in the smoke. Parkman will lead a team of soldiers into the tunnel carrying gas bombs and rifles. Seventeen wrecked cars lay between them and the mortally wounded creature in the tunnel. But they must get to the creature before he breaks the tunnel walls and causes a major flood. The suspense is genuine and joyfully sustained as the soldiers make their way deeper into the tunnel. The massive head of the mantis breaks through the shifting clouds. The soldiers fire their weapons, Parkman lobs gas bombs. The creature responds by tossing cars at them. Eventually the seemingly indestructible creature succumbs.

The rear projection, pyrotechnics, puppetry, music, art design and direction are flawless. Juran creates a sequence that rivals any in the pantheon of great science fiction/horror moments.

Mind you, this wasn't just any old fog. Universal effects technicians Fred Knoth and Orien Ernest won the Technical Achievement Academy Award in 1955 for developing their electric, hand portable, dry-oil fog machine. When Parkman and the mantis stalked each other, Knoth was on set bathing them in Oscar-winning fog.

In the modern era of instant gratification, these moments of suspense seem few and far between, but I don't feel that way. The very best of horror film history is not comprised of great films, but of great moments.

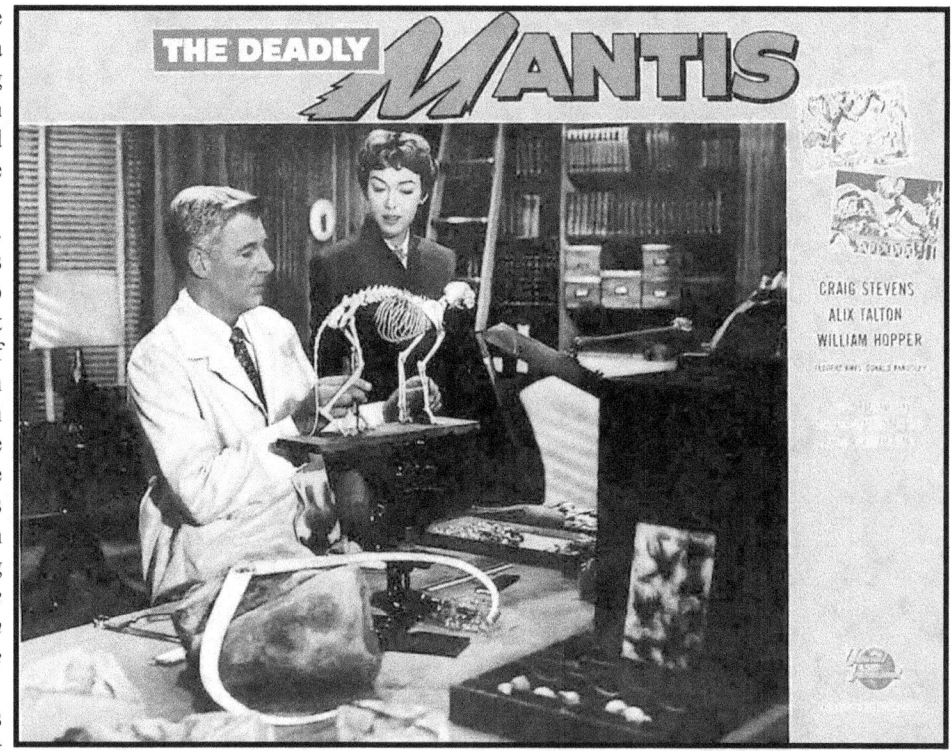

Dr. Jackson and Marge examine prehistoric bones to get an idea of how old the giant mantis may be.

Unsung heroes in this production are composers Irving Gertz and William Lava, who wrote the original music. As happened often with Universal, their names didn't appear on screen. Joseph Gershenson was head of U-I's music department for over 20 years and was credited as music supervisor on virtually every picture the studio released during that time. As with the editing and lighting, one of the score's most important functions was tying the film elements (documentary, stock footage and original material) together.

I'm hardly a musician, but I know what I like. Deep, ominous strings assist the viewer from one early clue to the next. Sweeping patriotic horns take us through military maneuvers and into battle against the beast once he's discovered. The composers seem to recognize they're working on a small film and, thankfully, avoid becoming too emphatic too often. Wisely, moments without music exist and there are moments when the droning buzz of the flying creature becomes the music itself.

While it shouldn't be surprising that one "big-bug" film would have similarities to another, outright theft probably should have been avoided. Berkeley lifted three scenes rather shamelessly from the bigger budgeted *Them!* While nothing's new under the sun, it's also true that if we're going to swipe from another film, then we should make ours better, or, at the very least, different. *The Deadly Mantis*, with versions of scenes scaled back for budgetary reasons, failed the test in two of the three examples.

An attack on a naval vessel, with ants ripping through the walls of the ship's radio room in the Warner Bros. classic, became an assault on an Italian fishing trawler in *The Deadly Mantis*. Wind machines, falling hawsers and debris hit the fisherman. Several cutaway shots to the flying Mantis puppet occur, including one so close that, unfortunately, the suspension wire

Scientist (Jackson), military officer (Parkman) and journalist (Blain) all shake hands, in a symbolic gesture that suggests mutual respect and collaboration and a willingness to get the job done right.

on the puppet's head is plainly visible. A final cutaway to the captain in the wheelhouse as the fishermen scream themselves into a blackout follows. While craftsmen made a valiant attempt, the final sequence did not compare to having the monsters right there on the set.

Remember the famed young Leonard Nimoy scene in *Them!*? He played an unnamed military office, who, in an effort to track the ants, collects wire stories and radio reports on unusual events around the country. This became Operation Marge in *The Deadly Mantis*. Marge suggests they track any incidents that seem out of the ordinary—a granary fire here, power lines down there. Ned scans a tickertape for odd occurrences while Marge makes notes on a map. The scenes accomplish the same thing, but the budget differences are painfully obvious.

In the third example, Berkeley actually redeems himself because *The Deadly Mantis* does do it better. In *Them!*, Onslow Stevens holds a press conference to tell the world about the ants. The general insists the public must be made aware and that they not panic. His speech, of course, is intercut with shots of folks becoming aware and starting to panic. The public plays no further part in *Them!* In *The Deadly Mantis*, Stevens holds a press conference to inform the Civil Ground Observers Corps about the mantis. Observers are told what to look and listen for and asked to report any unusual flying objects. It is the Ground Observers who locate the mantis and play a part in the resolution of the story. The press conference drives the story to its conclusion and is a better scene than the similar one in *Them!*

The Civilian Ground Observers Corps was very real: moms, dads, teachers, truck drivers all donating their time to "watch the skies." From 1949-58, over 800,000 volunteers manned 16,000 observation posts and 73 filter centers in what would come to be called Operation Skywatch. (The Canadian program lasted until 1965.) Observers studied wall charts and model airplanes to memorize the characteristics of our planes and "theirs," with procedures to report any sightings to the nearest filter center for dissemination to the military. The observers near my hometown had an unroofed plywood pen roughly six-feet square, unfurnished except for a telephone, situated atop the Community House. The Post's codename was Coco-Metro-Zero-Four-Roger. (I'm not making that up.) The regional Air Force filter center reported passing aircraft. People's fears, or if your prefer paranoias, were very real. The Ground Observer's Corps was gratefully acknowledged in *The Deadly Mantis*' credits.

Regardless of how much I enjoy *The Deadly Mantis*, the movie is not all sweetness and light. It is far from a perfect film.

First, there's Alix Talton. ("Alice" until she changed it in 1952.) Don't get me wrong! She was a former Miss Georgia, easy on the eyes, and she's an okay actress who had a steady career in television. But, clearly, her character has nothing to do. She weasels her way to the Arctic to "get a story" for the magazine she works for, and, other than taking two photographs at the site of the crashed C-47 (one of Steven's back), makes no further effort to get a story. To quote Carl Denham, she's there because, "the public, bless 'em, must have a pretty face to look at." She is Parkman's love interest in what ends up being an unimportant and none-too-interesting romantic subplot. And shame on the prop department for making her look as if she's not very bright. While discussing an upcoming magazine feature on the evolution of life beginning with the jelly fish (huh?), she is plainly seen holding a drawing of a giant squid. As knot-headed as this seems, it was still a missed opportunity for irony by writer Berkeley. Marge is reluctant at first to accept Ned's assertion of a giant insect, he could have reminded her of the giant squid in her very own article, surely proof creatures can grow to gigantic proportions in nature.

The character of Corporal (Paul Smith), the film's mandatory odious comic relief, is as annoying as they come. His, "Gosh, it's a girl! We've never seen a girl before" running gag is tiresome and cumulatively creates the film's weakest moments.

On a similar note, Lou the radar monitor (Phil Harvey) seems strangely exhausted and fed up with the search for the beast. It's an odd choice for Berkeley's script. Surely, their normal duties at the North Pole must get a bit dull. I would think a giant murdering insect would be an exciting, if not enjoyable, distraction. Universal's B-movie units kept Harvey busy, appearing in *Francis in the Haunted House, The Land Unknown, The Monolith Monsters, Monster on the Campus* and, as a state trooper, in *The Thing That Couldn't Die*.

A continuity error or two appear for idle gaffe spotters to hunt down, and the shadow of a microphone boom even makes a guest appearance in one scene. But if innocuous instances of this sort ruin the film for us, perhaps we're too hard to please anyway. The film's single biggest error is what's missing.

Sadly there are no shots of the mantis taking off or landing. The reason was pure economics. The production used a stalking mantis puppet that couldn't fly and a flying mantis puppet that could not extend its legs. That's all the producers could afford. Thus, landing was accomplished by a cut-away, a cessation of the droning flying sound effect and a quick cut back to the grounded or airborne monster (whichever the case may be). Seeing the beast land and takeoff would have added immeasurably to the attack sequences. In fact, a bit more destruction on the whole would have been welcome.

It must also be said it's unfortunate the film doesn't end immediately after the climactic battle in the tunnel. But it is a Hollywood film and they have to ensure the audience gets the happy ending.

Once the tunnel is cleared of smoke, we're shown the dead mantis amid the wreckage. Without the depth and atmosphere afforded by the dark and fog, the rear projected images are appallingly flat and the seams all too visible. Marge, suddenly a reporter again, must get a photo. Though dead, the creature's arm moves from an auto reflex mechanism and nearly swats Marge. She delivers a final, pointless, scream before Parkman rescues her. Ned snaps a photo of their kiss.

Ugh! Not only is it sappy and unbelievable and not only does it tie up subplots we never bought into and don't care about, but it is all accomplished with the worst series of process shots and traveling mattes in the entire picture. It's an awful conclusion to an otherwise worthy film.

Finally, a word about the pre-credit opening, a sequence no doubt added after the film's completion. Apparently, the filmmakers were concerned we wouldn't catch the two quick references to the beast's origin mentioned in the picture. So, they added a stock footage montage of a thunderous volcanic eruption near the South Pole, a reciprocating glacial upheaval near the North Pole and a narrator telling us, "For every action, there is an equal and opposite reaction." Then we get a quick, first glimpse of the monster. The sequence isn't necessary…but I like it.

First off; there's no beating around the bush. If the film is called *Jaws* it makes sense to keep your monster secreted away until the last suspenseful moment. But with a title like *The Deadly Mantis*…bring it on.

Secondly, the deep, oh-so-recognizable voice of the narrator, Paul Frees, is a boon. When a producer needed an authoritative or menacing voice in post-War Hollywood, their first call went to Frees, the Man of a Thousand Voices. Frees can be seen in a

number of classic genre films including *The Thing From Another World* and *War of the Worlds*, but we hear him in hundreds of radio shows, cartoons and many of the best-known pictures in fantasy film history, including: *When Worlds Collide, Earth Vs. The Flying Saucers, Rodan, The Time Machine, King Kong Escapes, The Absent-Minded Professor, The Abominable Dr. Phibes,* and on and on. My mouth waters just looking at the list of films I haven't mentioned. Personally, Frees scared the hell out of me when I was a child, providing as he did the voice of the evil, toy-hating Burgermeister Meisterburger from the animated *Santa Claus is Coming to Town*. When Frees is around, good things are happening for horror fans.

The Deadly Mantis is no classic, but there's a lot to like about it. It is a nifty, inexpensive thriller with a number of scenes that deserve to be remembered. Luckily, after too many years of obscurity, Universal released *The Deadly Mantis* to DVD in a boxed-set collection, along with *Dr. Cyclops, The Land Unknown, Leech Woman* and *Cult of the Cobra*. It's about time.

Ironically, the film *The Deadly Mantis* is in the same position as its marauding insect antagonist. It is a creature trapped in time. For generation X'ers and less open-minded viewers, it is dated and dull…but it has a cool monster. For those willing to give it its due, it is a museum-like slice out of time. The 1950s summed up in a 79-minute docudrama. The film features fear of the unknown, a unity of strangers watching the sky and a struggle to erect the perfect defense against a deadly, faceless attack.

Oh, and it's a pretty cool monster flick too.

MIDNIGHT MARQUEE BOOK REVIEW

by Gary J. Svehla

Bela Lugosi and Boris Karloff: The Expanded Story of a Haunting Collaboration by Gregory William Mank; McFarland www.mcfarlandpub.com Orders: 1-800-253-2187); $75 (hardcover)

In 1990 Gregory Mank saw the first version of this book published, an actual landmark in film criticism that helped cement Mank's importance as historian and critic. The hugely expanded and revised 2009 edition becomes the essential version to purchase. Yes, much of the additional information first appeared as articles in *Midnight Marquee* and *Monsters From the Vault* and others, but as gathered here in a beautifully bound McFarland edition, the book now seems definitive. I find myself questioning the philosophy of one writer constantly rewriting the same book (now the rage in monster kid fandom), but this book makes the point that any work of art is actually a work in progress, so revising the original manuscript is desirable for both the writer and fans alike. This edition makes the original 1990 version obsolete.

The text is sharper and more insightful than ever before, and Mank's style, almost that of a novelist, his dramatized style focused on cinematic criticism, is rather unique. One of my major concerns is the inclusion of non-collaborative movies such as *Murders in the Rue Morgue*, *The Mummy* and others, chapters or partial chapters that seem to exist simply because Mank expanded his research on these movies and wanted to find an excuse to work them in. Some may claim that these chapters give impressions of the "dynamic duo" in between collaborative productions, but at 685 pages selling for a whooping $75 (yes, the book contains a glossy color photographic section, but these posters have been reproduced, in color, many times before in the past), perhaps a slightly more focused and smaller tome would have been desirable.

Bela Lugosi and Boris Karloff has been well worth the wait, and it remains a definitive look at the careers of the two most important

horror film icons in cinema's history. The dialogue snaps and crackles, and Greg Mank appears to be having a deliciously obscene time tracing horror film history.

The Man Who Collected Psychos: Critical Essays on Robert Bloch, edited by Benjamin Szumskyj; McFarland www.mcfarlandpub.com Orders: 1-800-253-2187; $35 (softcover)

When I met Robert Bloch at the *Famous Monsters* Convention, I met one of the most unassuming celebrities ever. A group of friends, including Sue and me, took Mr. Bloch to lunch, and we spent a charming afternoon together. Bloch, modest and shy, would open up about any subject put to him. Here he was, one of the greatest writers of horror fiction, and he was almost ignored. Bloch, the author of *Psycho*, screenwriter of many classic horror movies, keeper of H.P. Lovecraft's mythos and author whose stories appeared on TV's *Thriller* is nothing less than iconic. But other than his own autobiography, precious little in the field of literary criticism exists to analyze his contributions to horror fiction and cinema, and Szumskyj's collection of essays gets the ball rolling.

Midnight Marquee contributor Steve Vertlieb writes the first chapter, combining a biography of the man's life with a quick appraisal of why this book exists in the first place. Vertlieb writes from the heart, and his decades-long letter writing friendship with Bloch fuels Vertlieb's passions. Happily, the book never allows itself to become stale or academic, and the essays are interesting and remain informative. We have pivotal essays on Bloch and H.P. Lovecraft, Bloch as humorist, the author's 1950s crime and suspense novels, an examination of Bloch's novel *The Scarf*, Bloch's *Psycho* trilogy, Bloch's partnership with Jack the Ripper, an examination of his serial killers and finally his television contributions, especially his work for *Alfred Hitchcock Presents*. Every aspect of his talent appears, and the book rushes by as we fill up on one topic and eagerly devour the next. For fans of classic horror and suspense fiction, television and cinema, the work of Robert Bloch deserves to be illuminated, and in this volume of collected essays, Bloch receives his just due.

Motion Picture Exhibition in Baltimore: An Illustrated History and Directory of Theaters, 1895-2004 by Robert K. Headley; McFarland www.mcfarlandpub.com Ordres: 1-800-253-2187; $65 (hardcover)

This book exists to serve two entirely different audiences. The first is those of us that grew up in Baltimore and remember the experience of first seeing, say, *Horror of Dracula* at the Colony Theatre on Harford Road, or watching *Forbidden Planet*, upon re-release, at the Waverly, near the old Memorial Stadium (home of the Baltimore Colts). Movie geeks remember the experience of being dropped off at the theater on a Saturday or Sunday afternoon, prepared to watch a double-feature (perhaps more than once), one fueled by sugary sodas, salty popcorn and chocolate candy. Sometimes the movie theater experience was more memorable than the films themselves. I remember at the Paramount the seats started very far from the theater screen, so it was always a thrill to get front row center seats there. However, at the narrow and long Arcade, the seats were so close to the screen that sitting in the front row would strain both the eyes and neck, so sitting a third of the way back was preferable. For those of us who haunted these downtown and neighborhood theaters for the decades of our youth, this book is a tribute for nostalgia's sake. Filled with photos and a detailed history of each theater, we can once again remember what these houses of the holy looked like during the 1950s and 1960s. For a movie buff such as me, this experience approaches the religious.

But what about those who did not grow up watching movies in Baltimore? Why would they buy this book? Well, an entire generation of movie palace geeks emerged, those dedicated fans who remember the classic posters, decor and architectural style of movie theaters that existed before the era of the multiplex and twinned cinema. The movie experience, at least for first-run movies, would occur downtown in art-deco theaters that also hosted live stage shows and big band concerts. For the second-run, these movies traveled to the suburbs, to the so-called neighborhood theaters, many of them almost as elaborate as the downtown houses. And for these urban movie dwellers, the magic palaces of Baltimore are not much different than similar theaters that existed in any major city across America. People remember when going to the movies was an event, an experience just as special as going to a concert or going to the theater.

For all these people and more, Robert K. Headley's book is a treasure-trove of fond remembrances. Again, the volume is heavily illustrated and the amount of research that fills over 500 pages is exhaustive. For anyone who remembers going to the movies during this classic movie era, this is a must-have book.

MIDNIGHT MARQUEE DVD REVIEWS

by Gary J. Svehla

Ratings: 4: Excellent; 3: Good; 2: Fair; 1: Poor

Frankenstein (75th Anniversary Edition)
Movie: 4.0; Disc: 3.5
[Universal]

After the initial DVD presentation and later the Legacy boxed set editions, why should fans purchase *Frankenstein* in this anniversary edition, knowing that within the next few years an HD upgrade should be available? Well, besides the wonderful packaging that houses the two disc edition, featuring new supplementals as well as a reissuing of old, the major reason to purchase this title again is that Universal took all the best of the past to feature the absolute best pressing of the original Universal classic, offered as a standalone movie on one disk without all the compression used in the past. Simply stated, *Frankenstein* has never looked or sounded better, and even if the 1931 early-sound creakiness remains, the audio seems far less scratchy. The soundtrack is more full-bodied and the density and clarity of the presentation is noticeably upgraded.

What is left to say about the movie and its presentation? Standout sequences are richer simply because of the improved picture clarity. In scenes featuring Colin Clive as Dr. Frankenstein speaking to his mentor Dr. Waldman (Edward Van Sloan), we can more fully focus on Clive's almost insane face and obsessive, piercing eyes that threaten to go over the top at any moment. Equally impressive is the ability to see where Van Sloan's hairpiece ends and actual hair begins. The initial graveyard sequence contains better contrast and the studio backgrounds are more impressive than ever. Fritz (Dwight Frye) climbing slowly up the gallows and cutting down the corpse, or the extended sequence showing Frankenstein and Fritz digging up the casket seem clearer and more haunting than ever. The miniature windmill at the end, though its special effect nature is more apparent, still looks grandiose with the irate villages lighting up the night with their torches. The watchtower with its high stonewalls and curving stairs appear more Gothic and impressive than ever before. And the sequences featuring Boris Karloff as the Monster never looked better and display Karloff's iconic silent-film performance (although the Monster's grunts seemed more distinct and provided a better segue to his even richer performance in *Bride of Frankenstein*) to perfection. His initial sequence, backing into the room, being caught in the beam of sunlight and reaching skyward with his arms elongated, is even more classic because the subtle lighting and cinematography is sharper and better detailed.

Karloff's makeup can be better appreciated because of the clarity and sharpness of the newly mastered DVD. Instead of finding flaws in makeup execution, this new clarity makes the Jack Pierce makeup even more superlative and breathtaking. Karloff's use of his hands and arms, whether they dangle or flex or are outstretched in front of him, help those of us who watched his performance for generations be better able to analyze why it works so well. The erect but bent forward stance, the use of his arms and the savagery in the mouth and eyes are all better seen and understood.

Many critics have always argued that Boris Karloff's performance as the Monster in *Frankenstein* was worthy of Academy Award Best Actor consideration, and this latest remastering of the classic demonstrates exactly why. Boris Karloff's Monster is great movie acting, period.

Most new extras are on the movie disc (the new commentary with Sir Christopher Frayling, *Karloff: The Gentle Monster* documentary featuring Steve Haberman, Greg Mank, Kim Newman, etc.) The best of the rest are on the second disc (which includes the TCM special *Universal Horror*, another documentary *The Frankenstein Files*, as well as a still and poster gallery). For a street price of under $20, this new version of *Frankenstein* is worth well having.

Imprint
Movie: 2.5; Disc: 3.5
[Anchor Bay]

Even though Showtime's *Masters of Horror* cable TV series (prematurely ended after its second season) has the latitude to depict hard-R movies with graphic violence and nudity, it refused to show bad boy Takashi Miike's *Imprint* as part of the series, and Anchor Bay is promoting this series reject as "banned from cable broadcast." And perhaps it should have been, although I am infinitely grateful that the mini-movie (63-minutes long… the return of the B feature!) is available on DVD for the discriminating fan.

First of all Miike is the gonzo Japanese director that crossed all barriers of good taste with movies such as *Audition, Ichi the Killer* and the *Dead or Alive* trilogy, all movies which stretch the perversity of what constitutes movie entertainment. *Imprint* is the type of movie fare that fascinates as it disgusts and nauseates. The viewer almost needs to take a shower after watching it because we feel dirty for observing sequences of ultra violent torture photographed as art. But Miike creates such a visual style, that at the same time that we feel disgusted, we are also fascinated and perhaps even impressed.

Imprint begins in 19th century Japan as a small boat courses through the night tides, illuminated by torches that find naked corpses floating in the river. Aboard is perennial B-actor Billy Drago, who is searching for the love of his life, a Japanese woman who has been sold into slavery and prostitution. Drago's lifetime obsession is to find her and marry her. Drago meets up with a disfigured prostitute, who purrs she will do whatever he wants to do with her this night. Sexual abandonment is the furtherest thing on his mind; what he wants is for the courtesan to share the knowledge she has of his lost love.

Told primarily in flashback, the courtesan worked with and knew the missing woman, who was accused of stealing the Madame's expensive ring and subjected to torture until she told the ring's location, but this now missing woman survives the most graphic torture possible (sharp needles are stuck into her toenails, into the gums of her mouth, etc.) until she apparently takes her own life. But as the story unfolds (the screaming Drago, wonderfully intense and over-the-top, does not believe this woman is telling the total truth and he demands she tell him everything), supernatural overtones appear as we see the courtesan is more a demonic spirit than an innocent bystander. This courtesan has a sister living in her skull in the form of a face in the center of a human hand that resides under her wig on the side of her head. And the sordid past of Drago's ladylove is revealed, Drago learning the poverty-stricken family had to survive by the guile of her mother performing abortions, with the younger girl dumping the dead fetuses into the river. The plot continues to go way over the top.

So after being subjected to sequences of graphic torture, the viewer is still bombarded with living arms existing in a disfigured woman's skull and fetuses being flushed down a river of death. While I was watching this movie for the first time a friend in absolute disgust walked out of the screening room, refusing to see more. *Imprint* is unsettling, although its direction, acting, period set design and cinematography are all outstanding. Perhaps it is the erotic element of this beautiful half-naked woman being tortured and ultimately strangled that is most disconcerting, but the violence depicted is deadly serious without an ounce of winking irony. Miike is a gifted filmmaker, yet he is also one twisted sick puppy, and it is difficult to answer whether one side balances out the other. In simple terms, *Imprint* is not for everyone and viewers should be warned of its unsettling nature.

Over three hours of supplemental extras appear, including interviews with Takashi Miike, and much more.

Gojira
Movie: 3.5; Disc: 4.0
[Classic Media]

At long last the original, uncut Japanese version of *Godzilla* is available on home video in a wonderfully remastered version (reissued in Blu-ray as well). The restoration is not up to Criterion standards, but the dense textures of the print, with deep blacks, is presented quite moodily. Speckling occurs occasionally to remind us of imperfections, but the look of the DVD is one of its strongest aspects, with an equally booming soundtrack (especially in the film's opening Japanese credits with the shrieks and thumps of Godzilla's impending attack). Unfortunately the American subtitles, done in yellow with a very thin font that becomes difficult to read overtop any light background, should have been corrected. A thicker, easier to read font should have been used, and in those sequences with a faster exchange of dialogue, sometimes the subtitled text changes faster than the human eye can read them. But this is a minor quibble.

Never has it become more apparent just how much Gojira/Godzilla is a metaphor for the technology of mass destruction, the atomic and hydrogen bomb! And in this Japanese version the morality of employing weapons of mass destruction becomes the keystone of the movie. Instead of being the schlocky giant-monster-on-the-loose that American audiences got in the recut/redubbed Raymond Burr version (also available on the second disc for comparison), *Gojira* becomes a tale of profound emotion and moral ambiguity. *Gojira* is never a fun-filled special effects kiddy matinee romp; it is a dark, brooding drama of human emotion that just happens to feature a radioactive beast from the ancient past running amok. But *Gojira* offers so much more.

The movie focuses upon four people: the wizened scientist who wants to study, not kill, the beast (Professor Tanabe); Emiko, the beautiful love interest and daughter of the professor; Ogata, the young hero who wishes to save the world by destroying Gojira, but he also wants to marry Emiko and his position toward the beast alienates him from the professor; and Serizawa, the disfigured youthful scientist who holds the key to the weapon that can kill Gojira, but he fears this weapon of mass destruction could fall into the wrong hands! Just like the Robert Corthwaite character from *The Thing*, Professor Tanabe ignores the death and destruction caused by the rampaging Gojira, the monster's radioactive breath melting people and property alike. He sees the reanimation of this prehistoric creature as the scientific find of the century and he wishes to learn why the beast is still alive. Serizawa, one side of his face scarred and an eye patch hiding a missing eye, is a Japanese victim of WWII nine years earlier (the movie was released in 1954), perhaps even a survivor of the two atomic bombings. He has invented an Oxygen Destroyer machine that melts the flesh of all living sea creatures in close proximity th the device. The weapon, as deadly as the atomic bomb, could fall into the wrong hands and be used to destroy not only sea life, but life outside the water's rim. He is morally conflicted...he holds the key to save Japan from the ravages of Gojira, but if his documentation is found, or if he is captured and tortured, his weapon could mean the end of civilization. So the angst-ridden Serizawa at first consents to show his machine to Emiko, but he swears her to silence. She, also morally conflicted, breaks her promise and tells Ogata. Still refusing to allow his weapon to be used to kill the monster, Serizawa finally burns his papers and allows the technology to be used to destroy Gojira, but in the best sense of sacrifice, while submerged underwater in a diver's suit, the scientist cuts his air hose and takes his life, making sure he will never be captured and forced to divulge his secretes. After Gojira dies, so does Serizawa, sacrificing his life so such a weapon will never be used again.

And then we have the star of the show, Gojira, the monster who never looks ridiculous, and who never appears to be a man in a monster suit. The monster, whether emerging from the sea (or at first being seen only as an atomic glow beneath the water, where it preys on ships), or lurking, mostly hidden, over the top of mountain peaks, or stomping his way through fishing villages, the slow-moving beast dominates the movie when his back fin radiates and glows and his atomic breath shoots from his mouth and melts anything in his path. The photography is always dark-lit and ominous. Even an homage to *King Kong* occurs, with a train being derailed by Gojira, and the monster chewing one of the train carriages and throwing the twisted metal to the ground below.

Gojira, for those who only saw *Godzilla*, is an eye-opener, a movie rich in philosophy, moral ambiguity and angst. It is a special-effects monster-movie marvel, but then again it is so much more, so much richer. It is definitely a movie classic and one of the best cinematic reactions to the dropping of atomic weapons on Japan at the end of WW II. Extras include the more familiar Americanized re-cut version (quality not as good as *Gojira*), an insert book with a wonderful essay by Steve Ryfke, two documentaries, trailers and an audio commentary.

The Descent
Movie: 3.0; Disc: 3.5
[Lionsgate]

Horror films seldom garner the critical raves and mainstream notice that Neil Marshall's *The Descent* earned over the course of the past few years (the film was released in Europe a year before the U.S.A.). Readers of *MidMar* can remember the enthusiastic kudos I gave to Marshall's first feature film, *Dog Soldiers*, one of the best modern horror films (and best werewolf movies ever), bar none. That direct-to-DVD release stood heads and tails above most of the other horror movie releases back in 2002, but now *The Descent* ups the ante.

Neil Marshall, with *The Descent*, wanted to pay tribute to the formula horror movies that he most loves from the 1970s, including *The Texas Chain Saw Massacre*, but here he also transcends the formula and that's why his second film seems so impressive and resonates long after leaving the theater. *The Descent*, both written and directed by Marshall, has many strengths in its favor, but a few nagging flaws intrude, unfortunately.

Let me explain.

The movie's structure, running a tight 99 minutes, features an all female cast of adventurers who live their life to the extreme (three women are shown white water rafting during the opening credits). After a horrifying tragedy strikes one member of the close-knit group, they gather together one year later to give moral support to Sarah, the victim of the automobile tragedy, and to explore some supposedly safe caves. The sequence leading up to "the descent" is fairly typical, showing the diverse group (the younger and older sister, the gung-ho leader, the punked-out extremist, the quiet one, etc.) bonding, allowing Marshall to develop insightful characters in minimal time. However, once these 20-something ladies don their helmets and rugged terrain garb, they become difficult to distinguish, and once they enter the realm of total darkness down below, keeping everyone straight becomes a challenge. But basically the three-four main explorers are fairly easily distinguished.

At the centerpiece of the movie is the tragically sad (and medicated) Sarah, who was a front seat passenger in a vehicle driven by her distracted husband (subtle hints occur that the husband is having an affair with Sarah's friend Juno), which veered across the center lane heading directly into the path of another van. In rapid fire intensity, metallic poles from the van penetrate the front windshield of Sarah's car killing both her husband and baby daughter. Sarah feels responsible, yet she was merely a chatting passenger when fate took over. The cave exploring "girls-week-out" becomes cathartic for Sarah and helps her heal emotionally. So from the get-go *The Descent* establishes complex relationships that cut deeper than the typical horror excursion. Especially now that Juno and Sarah are reunited for the first time since the accident and the question of infidelity intensifies.

The cinematography of *The Descent*, orchestrated by Sam McCurdy, becomes a major strength of the movie. Four sequences from the movie dominate and major character interaction develops from those sequences. The first is the automobile collision at the beginning with the slightly slow-motion metal rods penetrating the front windshield and killing two occupants by impaling them. The second is a sequence, one year later, with the walking-wounded Sarah staring outside the window in the rural cabin as a metal rod breaks through the window, startling both Sarah and the audience, but the shock sequence establishes itself quickly as only a horrible flashback of Sarah's past tragedy. The third sequence is a sequence in the cave where the too cavalier Juno uses her physical prowess to kill a crawler (the name for the underground species of flesh-eating monsters), and after being startled, immediately afterwards, she uses one of her metal hooks to stab one of her human girlfriends through the throat, dropping her to her knees, and then abandoning her for dead, even though speechless, she is still alive (but near death). [Spoiler alert!] The fourth sequence is the movie's final one, deep in the caves, with Sarah, dazed, wide-eyed and obviously out of her mind, kneeling over a birthday cake, the image of her still-alive daughter smiling and looking down at her cake.

The automobile accident image is related to the follow-up one of her awakening in her hospital bed, tubes connected to her body, her face bruised and cut. Sarah, panicking, rips out the connecting wires and tubes and runs, full throttle, down the hospital corridor, trying to outrun sections of the corridor that grow dark before she outruns them. Finally colliding with one of her friends, Sarah crumbles to the ground, sobbing, grasping her friend, while gurneys and medical staff avoid, ignore and duck around her as the grieving, injured woman sobs hysterically in the middle of the corridor. The fact that in one cruel sweep of fate she lost both her husband and only child hits her square in the face. And the fact that she feels responsible makes the tragedy all the worse. Thus guilt, anger and redemption become the major themes the movie explores, while at the same time her friends try to overcome feelings of guilt for abandoning their friend by trying to return everything to former normalcy by a communal return to extreme life adventures.

The second vision of Sarah, alone, staring outside the window, and getting pierced by the unexpected metal rod penetrating the glass window, is only a dream, a flashback...perhaps even a

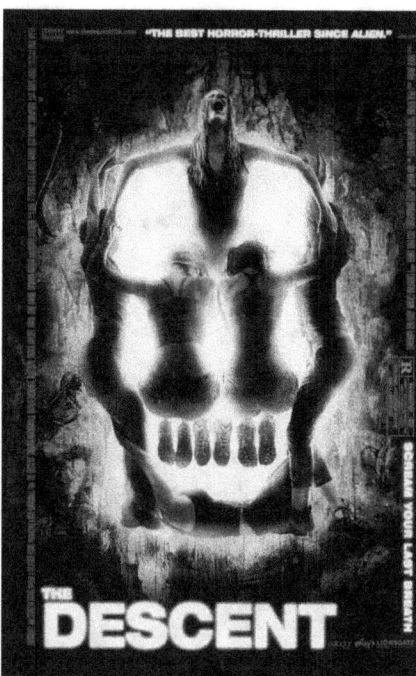

cheap horror film shock. But the sequence resonates because it demonstrates that Sarah, reaching for her prescription medicine at one crucial sequence, is prone to delusions and flashbacks that seem lifelike and current. In other words, her damaged mental state and fragile grip on reality is established.

The third image of the irresponsible leader Juno accidentally but mortally wounding a companion by thrusting a metal spike in her throat becomes a metaphor for Sarah's moral anguish. Both women acted accidentally (Sarah comments to her husband that he seems distant in the final seconds before the car crash, and so she feels responsible for distracting him) but both are responsible for killing people they both love. Sarah, who awakens in a hospital bed, was unable to come to the aide of her loved ones. But Juno, who is shocked and horrified by her mistake, leaves her friend to die, guilt ridden from failing to act responsibly. During the climax, after Sarah becomes unhinged mentally, she jabs a metal pike into Juno's leg after confronting her, having found the body of the now dead companion. In her mind Sarah is able to assuage her own guilt by avenging the death of a mutual friend killed by the very woman that so recklessly doomed this group of friends, taking them down an unexplored cave after promising they would be exploring a cave already surveyed and considered safe. Also, if her husband was having an affair with Juno, Sarah's revenge is now complete.

The fourth and final image is a culmination of many things. After Sarah, in her deluded state, images herself escaping

from the caves (and the image of her grasping for breath, breathing in fresh air, as she pushes herself out of the cave, the cave's exit covered by tree branches and green vegetation, is another iconic image, this time serving as a birth metaphor) and running into her van, as she speeds out onto the main highway, she pulls the car over to the side of the road, but part of the vehicle extends onto the highway. In a twisted sense the viewer is always looking into the backseat thinking that Marshall might succumb to the cliché of having one of the crawlers hiding there. However, while we are anticipating the crawler's appearance, outside the back window, blurred at first, is a huge truck that comes bellowing down the highway, its horn blowing as it passes Sarah's vehicle. Flashing back to the automobile accident from the beginning of the film, the audience becomes intensely fearful because we suspect the large truck will ram Sarah's vehicle and end the movie as it began. Around this point the American theatrical version ends, but the director's cut takes us back down into the cave to the final haunting sequence with Sarah, her daughter and the birthday cake. Sarah's mind, totally gone, images that her daughter is alive with her down in these catacombs of horror. At least they are together again. On this bleak note the movie ends.

Neil Marshall's produces layers upon layers of psychological baggage that takes *The Descent* (a descent into madness?????) on a rather complex trip for a horror programmer. However, the psychological horror and imagery of the movie's first half (the crawlers do not enter the movie until about 55 minutes in) out-shocks the claustrophobic pursuit by the monstrous crawlers during the movie's final 45 minutes. In fact, after about 20 minutes of such repetitive horror attacks, the film loses a tad of its momentum (just a tad, mind you!). In wondrously photographed underground sequences, Marshall allows Sarah to enter an underground pool that is backlit in glowing red. When the monster emerges from the water and the two fight to the death, the photography is so dark that the audience will most likely have difficulty following all the action. And while the action is fast and brutal, Marshall cuts the action in a style approximating Ridley Scott's filming of the action sequences in *Gladiator* (sped up action with herky-jerky edits that heighten the tension by creating an almost strobing affect with the pitch dark underground lit by illumination from flashlights and helmet lights).

Even with such minor flaws, *The Descent* becomes a superior horror movie with a deeply psychologically-crafted script that features strong characterization. Yes, Marshall succumbs to that old cliché of the snapshot of the entire group in happier times that plays over the end credits, but very few missteps of that sort occur. The extras on the DVD are voluminous and insightful, especially the on-screen interview with Neil Marshall. But along with *Dog Soldiers* and now *The Descent*, Neil Marshall is emerging as an original talent of well-crafted horror film entertainment. While *The Descent* is far from perfect, it is an immensely well made horror film that dares to make us both think and feel, all punctuated by intense visuals focusing on frightened women squeezing through underground passages in pitch-darkness pursued by cannibalistic monsters that feed upon their flesh. This is the stuff of which nightmares are made! And great horror movies!

**Masters of Horror:
Dario Argento's Pelts**
Movie: 2.5; Disc: 3.5
[Anchor Bay]

The first season of Showtime's *Masters of Horror* featured Dario Argento's haunting episode *Jenifer*, one of the series' best mini-movies, a film that was both erotic and terrifying, fueled by a strong script. In the second season Argento returns directing *Pelts*, a mini-movie as bad as *Jenifer* was good. In fact, *Pelts* symbolizes just about everything that is wrong with the modern horror movie. The story is more a premise or thesis—suppose all those horrible things hunters do to their animal prey could be done to humans, how would we like it? Thus, the episode focuses on the technical makeup effects created by Howard Berger and Gregory Nicotero, which features close-ups of faces sliced in half by steel traps, the human skull smashed in by a baseball bat (with some flies licking the corpse thrown in for good measure) and Meat Loaf Aday's character Jake taking a knife and skinning the dead man's torso, offering his flesh to his stripper lover. The overall effect here is to ogle and squirm at the nasty effects, which are most cleverly conceived. To drive the metaphor home, in the beginning Larry finds a trap housing the bloody leg of a raccoon that escaped by chewing off its own leg. At the end, stripper Shana (Ellen Ewusie) gets her arm crushed in an elevator, but from fear and panic, she rips her arm free as the bloody stump bleeds profusely. The hunter becomes the hunted, but the message is blatant and lacks subtlety.

Secondly, while *Jenifer*'s sexuality was hot and bothersome, the sex here is sleazy and asexual. We have strippers writhe and shake their assets, a few lap dances erupt and Meat Loaf gets to mount Shana in a visual turnoff that is almost painful to watch. Eroticism has been replaced by exploitative and aggressive sexual acts, acts of sex that are not titillating in the least.

What works well in *Pelts* is the cinematography by Attila Szalay, controlled by the visual eye of Argento. The final elevator death sequence, bathed in blacks and reds, works best when shot from a distance and the mayhem is more a flicker than a sustained gander. The foggy moment where the magical raccoons are captured, the old hag's shack in the background, is a visual tour de force. Even the manner in which the shimmering pelts, hanging in the cellar of John Saxon's (he plays the old hillbilly geezer) house, become almost mesmerizing. Also, the beautiful, haunting score by frequent Argento collaborator Claudio Simonetti, accented by an even more haunting female voice, becomes a musical score too classy for its subject matter.

The aging Meat Loaf Aday does a fine job in his stereotypical performance, as does John Saxon playing an old hillbilly poacher. But for an artist as gifted and subtle as Dario Argento, perhaps the script offered him, based upon a story by F. Paul Wilson, was simply bad. Argento at his best does terrify his audiences, and the director never avoids showing scenes of torture and bloodshed. But in Argento's best, such sequences of mayhem, blood and death always contained a style, a poetry and a sense of art. Here

Argento becomes the little kid in the playground enjoying creating a tapestry of bloodshed simply to shock his audience.

Few artful sequences remain, too many sequences exist of technical makeup effects that gross us out more than terrify. *Pelts* is worse than simply being bad Argento. *Pelts* squanders Argento's art, and Argento himself is the one responsible for subjugating his creative powers.

The Mario Bava Collection Volume 1
Movies: *Black Sunday* (4.0);
Black Sabbath (3.0);
The Girl Who Knew Too Much (3.5);
Kill, Baby, Kill (3.0)
Disc: 4.0; Disc: 3.5
[Anchor Bay]

For quite some time the original releases of *Black Sunday* and *Black Sabbath* on DVD, from Image, have been out of print. So it is refreshing to see an entire Mario Bavo boxset, all movies remastered, released at a very fair price, housing five Bava masterworks (three of which are reviewed).

Black Sunday made my list as one of the 13 most influential horror movies ever made, and here's the reason why. Unlike the current Technicolor British Hammer horrors of the mid-1950s, Mario Bava went back to Universal of the 1930s to create the look and feel of *Black Sunday* (here called *The Mask of Satan*, its British release title, uncut, containing the original musical score that AIP replaced with the Les Baxter version), with the Hammer gore added to remind us that this was 1960. Many of Bava's well-manicured outdoor sets, created on interior soundstages, remind audiences more than a little of the similar outdoor-created-indoor soundstage sets from *Frankenstein* and *Bride of Frankenstein*. Mario Bava, who also photographed the movie, wanted to control every camera movement, every flicker of light, every shadow, every tree and every aspect of the set design. And to watch *Black Sunday* is to watch iconic cinematography, among horror cinema's best ever. Even though Bava was also a great director, it's the audacious visual world created in the movie that garners the most respect from me.

Even though we are not sure whether we are dealing with actual vampires or soul-corrupted denizens of the undead, resurrected via witchcraft, *Black Sunday* features two sequences of sheer visual beauty—and horror. When their carriage is being repaired, doctors Gorobec (John Richardson) and Kruvajan (Andrea Checchi) stumble upon a nearby burial vault, containing a huge stone sarcophagus with a clear pane of glass directly above the corpse's head, where a metal-spiked mask has been pounded onto her face. This underground sequence begins as the camera takes a 360-degree pan around the magnificent set, beginning and ending focused on the fascinated human onlookers. A stone crucifix rests above the glass pane to keep this demonic women in her coffin. Of course when the younger Gorobec drifts away, the elder Kruvajan remains alone to be attacked by a deftly photographed (more shadow and quick cut) giant bat. During the fight for life, the doctor uses his cane to kill the bat, but he accidentally smashes the glass in the coffin. Unfortunately the doctor sustains a cut on his hand where droplets of blood spill upon the corpse's face. The doctor leaves, but the viewer sees that the corpse's eyes begin to reform, as the witch returns slowly to life.

Later in the movie, one of horror cinema's most impressive sequences occurs. After dark a young village girl ventures alone to the barn to milk a cow (in a sequence bearing a strong resemblance to Val Lewton's similar scene from *The Leopard Man*). She looks outside a rectangular cut in the barn, which draws the camera both toward the hole and quickly outside (the young girl meanwhile returns to her cow). The camera continues to pan in on a disturbed grave whose displaced earth is slowly breaking apart. Extended, clawing arms rise from below and force their way to freedom. The reanimated corpse yanks off his metal-spiked face mask, similar to the one seen earlier by the two doctors. This vampire/witch, the brother of the dead witch Asa (Barbara Steele), soon is riding a slow-motion carriage through the woods (interestingly, shots of the driver Igor whipping his horses are photographed in regular motion, while the carriage drifts hauntingly in slow motion along through the forest). The carriage stops to pick up Dr. Kruvajan, who thinks he is being taken to Prince Vajda's castle to treat the stricken elder, but in reality, he is being taken to that castle's underground burial vault, housing witch Asa. In a wonderful sequence Igor leads Kruvajan through the Prince's castle, behind a huge fireplace into the hidden passageways beyond. Kruvajan stumbles further and further behind, having only the lantern of Igor to guide him. In a

terrifying sequence, the doctor reaches the lantern that is now suspended in mid-air. The lantern drops unexpectedly and breaks. Kruvajan arrives at the familiar burial vault and is left alone. In a scene similar to the Jonathan Harker burial vault sequence from *Horror of Dracula*, both characters (Harker and Kruvajan) try to storm up the steps to freedom, but both find the vault door closed. Defeated, terror in their eyes, they are forced to once again descend the stone steps to their doom. Kruvajan stands transfixed as the burial vault at first rumbles violently, shakes and then explodes. The stone walls break away revealing the undulating, squirming, heaving chest of the reanimated witch queen, huge spike holes in her face, her fully formed eyes wide open and terrifying to behold. Her arms stretch out along her side, and her pointed fingernails scrap against the stone sarcophagus. Using her mesmeric powers, Asa demands that Kruvajan approach her and kiss her lips, and she will suck the life from him. But instead of death, a vampiric state of undead will result and he will become Asa's slave. This entire sequence is classic horror in both mood and visual content. The camera angles, the sweeping pans, the artistically rendered subtle zooms and the acting all combine to produce a sequence that lingers in the imagination.

These sequences, together with Asa's pre-credit execution, the intense scenes showing the slow decline and death of Prince Vajda, the slower transformation of innocent Katia (Steele in a dual role) into the demon witch and her faster transformation back, the spooky appearances of Igor, the spike-in-the-eye dispatch of those possessed by the witch or her brother, etc. create a true classic of the horror genre and a film that influenced Euro-horror for generations.

The importance of *Black Sunday* cannot be argued, as it has become one of the most important horror movies of the 1960s. The pristine mastering presented here is as good if not better than the Image version, and the audio commentary by Tim Lucas entertains and educates. Multiple trailers and a still and poster gallery are included. However, the only negative is the lack of a non-dubbed original Italian version with subtitles, and it might have been nice to include the American AIP dubbed version to compare to the British version used. But this one title makes the box set an essential must-have purchase.

Next up is *Black Sabbath*, a movie radically different in its original Italian version compared to the reedited version distributed in the U.S. by American International. Too bad the AIP version was not included, for it features the voice of Boris Karloff, while the Italian subtitled version re-dubs the icon's voice. In the AIP version the trilogy (the Italian title is *Three Faces of Fear*) has been reshuffled with *The Drop of Water* first, *The Telephone* second and *The Wurdalak* third (to build to the Karloff entry).

In the Bava original, the weakest story, *The Telephone*, is first, *The Wurdalak* second and *The Drop of Water*, the most terrifying tale, comes last, where it rightfully belongs. *The Telephone* plays longer in the Bava original since the subplot involves a lesbian undertone that AIP wanted to eliminate, to appeal to the teeny-bopper horror trade of 1963. However, AIP dropped the delightful end coda that is featured here…Karloff in narrator mode, dressed in his Wurdalak makeup and costume, delivering the farewell message, as the camera pulls away showing that Karloff is striding a phony hobby-horse, with crew people running quickly and all around Karloff, creating the illusion that the speeding horse is running past trees and shrubs, as the cinematographer sits behind the camera and lights create the gloomy mood shining on blue backdrops. The ending is fabulous because it both reveals and debunks the magic of moviemaking, showing the craft behind the illusion.

Never having been a fan of anthology horror movies, *Black Sabbath* is indeed one of the best and its Technicolor photography contrasts nicely with the stark monochrome tones of Bava's debut three years earlier. *The Telephone* is slight compared to the other two entries, but its importance the vehicle that helped establish the giallo genre cannot be downplayed. Here we have a beautiful woman who returns home to her apartment, undresses, and starts getting threatening phone calls from a deep-voiced person who states he loves her body, he is watching her and she will be dead by dawn, strangled to death. The story develops that the caller is the victim's former female lover, rejected and sent away, and now the jilted woman wants to terrify the young woman as an act of revenge. However, the terrified victim phones her abuser (not knowing this fact) and asks her to come over to offer security. Burying a kitchen knife under her pillow, both women are surprised by the victim's male lover, who is now out of prison and also wants to get both women (perhaps their lesbian affair broke off his relationship with the victim). Before the movie ends, the lesbian phone abuser is strangled and the feisty female victim uses the hidden knife to stab and kill her male attacker. All the giallo cinematic themes and camera tricks are here and *The Telephone* becomes important for introducing many of them to mainstream audiences.

The Wurdalak comes closest in mood to *Black Sunday*, once again featuring fog-shrouded indoor sets approximating the great Russian outdoors. The night sky is constantly bathed in dark blue tones, with shadowy set-pieces dripping with dank horror. Karloff's performance is more a look, a stuttering walk and a dead face with intense, penetrating eyes. He is Gorca, the patriarch of his family, consisting of his children and their spouses/lovers and their children. When a corpse is found beheaded, with a knife in the creature's back, son Valdimire (Mark Damon) knows that a Wurdalak (or vampire) is stalking the area. The knife belongs to his father and, if the elder does not return within two hours, the family knows that Gorca has become a Wurdalak himself. The film's theme is one that would be best explored in a feature format. One by one each family member succumbs to the love of a family member infected by vampirism, foolishly putting one's guard down. Innocent family members are victimized and transformed into a family of Wurdalaks. Finally in the film's final moments, Valdimire succumbs to the charms of his sexy blonde girlfriend, herself bitten, who in turn bites her lover in the neck, as the family of vampires watch through the window panes outside the home. It is a mesmerizing sequence demonstrating that the love of family is stronger than even the love of life. Again, that intriguing theme dominates, becoming slightly lethargic because of its over reliance on the mood of dread.

Finally *The Drop of Water*, 20 minutes of extreme Bava cinematography and mood, expertly directed, becomes the shining segment of this trilogy. Simply stated, an old woman psychic dies while conducting a séance, and two women have to prepare her for burial. One of the two women steals the expensive ring from her dead finger, and a buzzing fly that lands on the finger, once the ring is removed, creates an aura of terrifying horror. The woman's frigid, horrifying face, frozen in death with eyes open, only adds to the sense of fear. We follow the woman who steals the ring as she returns home and the buzzing fly follows her, but now a methodically dripping faucet only adds to the rhythm of terror generated. Before long the woman's corpse appears in a rocking chair and flashing lights create a truly cinematic exercise in ultimate horror that has never been better executed by Mario Bava. This sequence is worthy of a tight 20-minute running time, and while the equally short *The Wurdalak* seems excessive, *The Drop of Water* seems just right.

Again, anthology horror movies are not my forte, but *Black Sabbath* (aka *The Three Faces of Fear*), along with *Dead of Night*, are the best. Not nearly as effective as *Black Sunday*, *Black Sabbath* (the U.S. re-titling purposely trying to cash in on the earlier Bava classic) is nonetheless a testament to the newly blossoming Euro-horror imports and the directorial/cinematographic expertise of the legendary master, Mario Bava.

Surprisingly, *The Girl Who Knew Too Much* (1963), reedited and rescored and released in America as *The Evil Eye* by American International, remains my second favorite Bava film. Even though it helped to create the giallo genre of thriller-mystery-murders, usually with sharp objects, *The Girl Who Knew Too Much* remains horrifying in both tone and cinematography. Heavily influenced by Hitchcock, this thriller contains all those stylistic touches that make Bava great. Instead of opting for period detail, this final black-and-white Bava classic transports us to the 20th century in every way. The movie begins as our sexy heroine Nora Davis (Leticia Roman) is aboard a plane ready to land in Rome. However, before she lands safely she becomes involved with a drug dealer, who gives her a pack of marijuana joints disguised as cigarettes, and she inadvertently smokes one. A bombastic and brassy 1960s-style pop song becomes the theme song that reoccurs throughout the movie. We are no longer in the Gothic Bava-land we normally visit.

The movie gets off to a spectacular start as Nora goes to the home of her aunt, who is attended by youthful Dr. Bassi (John Saxon), who seems quite concerned about the elder woman's health. That very night, in a sequence similar to *The Drop of Water* segment from *Black Sabbath*, the woman has an attack and dies, her eyes wide open and her face frozen in death, as her pet yanks at her bed clothes, rocking the corpse back and forth. In a panic and unable to phone the hospital, Nora, naked under her shiny raincoat, runs down the Plaza stone steps, illuminated by glaring overhead lights and mist, and is first stalked and then attacked by a purse-snatcher, who throws the girl to the ground, knocking her unconscious. Soon awakening, Nora, groggy and disoriented, sees a young girl in obvious distress slowly extend her arms in a silent cry for help. As this girl falls to the ground, we see a huge butcher knife embedded in her bloody back, as Nora watches from the shadows. A mysterious man comes across the girl, looks around to be sure he is not being watched, pulls the knife out of her back, throws it away and carries the body back into the fog. Next this mysterious man, who has been shadowing the mysterious but now dead woman, attempts to revive the again unconscious Nora by shaking her and pouring whisky down her throat. Nora awakens in a hospital bed surrounded by the angelic white caps of the nurses. The fantastic opening sequence, shot on location in Rome, features Bava's intensely controlled cinematography, tense editing and effective acting delivered by the expressive Leticia Roman.

While most movies are lucky to have one intense centerpiece sequence, *The Girl Who Knew Too Much* has at least three. A second classic suspense moment occurs on a night that Nora is staying alone in the home of a newfound friend. She is afraid of being surprised by the serial killer, so she uses a ball of twine to booby trap the apartment. She flings talcum power everywhere to make the floors slippery and the cord will trip any intruder and awaken her in the process. However, as soon as she reclines in her bed, the huge translucent windows reveal a shadowy stalker, who walks around the perimeter of the house, eerily trying to find an open window or door. The woman gasps for breath and breathes heavily as she watches the fiend attempt to break into the house.

Finally, Nora receives instructions to come alone to an apartment where she is informed all will be revealed. The girl takes a cab to the high rise (the sequence includes a beautiful panning shot at night as the cab drives up to the entrance) and Nora goes inside, not realizing another car pulls up right behind her and an unknown person follows her into the building (some beautiful point-of-view subjective shots mirror the slasher genre 15 years later). Nora enters a noisy metal elevator that carries her upward in darkness. Once outside the elevator, she continues to walk up deserted staircases, lit by ambient light and shadow. She walks into an open, unoccupied apartment and glares down hallways that contain naked lights swaying in the breeze. Nora then hears a voice that tells her not to be afraid, to come on in. Bava treats this Lewton-esque "walk" with all the tension and horror that can be generated. As the girl, almost too afraid to walk ahead but too afraid to turn back, musters the courage to keep going further down toward the very end of the corridor. About to enter this final room, Nora panics as the lights suddenly go out. Bravely, she is about to enter the dark room, but she momentarily swoons as a dark male figure creeps up behind her, and she turns and starts to punch and slap him. The audience recognizes the male intruder as Dr. Brassi, Nora's savior, who is simply following her to protect her. After she scratches the doctor's face, she comes to her senses and finally recognizes her boyfriend. Bassi turns on the light in the room and Nora

finds a tape recorder running, which features the mysterious voice she heard when first entering the room. This leads her to the conclusion of her frightened journey.

On the audio commentary author Tim Lucas informs us that *The Girl Who Knew Too Much* was Bava's least successful production, but the movie is a bonafide classic. Withoutt financing from AIP, Bava's budgets dwindled and the director would seldom work with these large budgets and quality stars in the future.

The Man and the Monster
Movie: 3.0; Disc: 3.5
[Casa Negra]

Oh, those Latinos!

Seldom has the concept of tragic hero (in the truest Shakespearean sense) been better evoked then in this Mexican horror movie, made in 1958. This film is another Abel Salazar production, starring Salazar, directed by Rafael Baledon (who also directed *The Curse of the Crying Woman*) and featuring mood-evoking cinematography by Raul Martinez Solares. The story, a clever combination of the Faust legend with a tad of *Dr. Jekyll and Mr. Hyde* included, demonstrates how important pathos and a tragic flaw become to the success of the best horror thrillers.

The second greatest pianist in the world, Samuel Magno (Enrique Rambal), desires to be the greatest at any cost, including selling his soul to Satan. A portrait of the greatest living pianist, Alejandra, hangs in his house, but her rotting corpse, holding a special piece of music clutched in her hand, is stored in the side room. Magno mentors a Alejandra look-alike, Laura (both characters played by Martha Roth), to prepare her for her debut recital in a few days. Magno rants that she will be declared the best in the world! By night, protected by his mysterious mother Cornelia (Ofelia Guilmain), Magno locks himself in his house, throws the keys outside and plays a special piece of music that turns him into a ferocious werewolf, actually something akin to a were-terrier (with a huge golf ball-size nose that would impress W.C. Fields). This makeup becomes the film's most obvious misstep (although the werewolf looks silly, the fiend is one step above *The Brainiac*). Unable to escape, Magno plays his heart out, but by the film's second half, the feral musician manages to transform outside the safety of his home and runs amok in several key sequences. In one dramatic scene, Magno goes to the hotel room of Ricardo (Salazar), a music journalist and fan of Magno, to kill him. Inside the room he instead finds an innocent victim on the bed, and the werewolf literally picks up the screaming man, holds him over his head and throws the rag doll onto the bed, collapsing the piece of furniture. Unknown to Magno, Ricardo has been moved to another room. However, all Hell erupts in the hotel lobby as the desk manager and Ricardo try to combat the monster. In a large soundstage set, this hotel lobby more closely resembles an airport, with the monster running at breakneck speed at the desk clerk, with both the clerk and Ricardo doing flips and pratfalls breaking furniture. It's a dazzling battle royale.

The film's most impressive cinematography involves a dual layer montage of monster Magno's quivering face, with fire burning behind him, merging with a shot of his hated rival Alejandra.

In another amazing sequence, Magno sneaks back to Alejandra's dressing room, where he slashes her throat with a pair of scissors lying on her dressing table. And without notice, Magno carries her dying, blood-dripping body to his own home, where he places her corpse in a chair in a small side room, next to the opulent living room, which houses his piano. There she begins to rot, holding the devilish sheet music in her hand, music that Magno tries to burn unsuccessfully. Then, at his leisure, at night, he can open the door and play his music, watching his dead rival who is powerless to do anything. Sequences of the manic musician playing feverously in his werewolf makeup are quite compelling.

Of course the movie's climax occurs at Laura's recital, where Magno conducts the orchestra. Of course when she plays the devil's music, from the sheet music that still has not been destroyed, Magno transforms into the werewolf in plain sight of Laura, Ricardo and the audience. Within seconds the beast is shot dead by the authorities in the audience.

While *The Man and the Monster* might not be the finest Mexican horror movie ever made, it remains an above average one that transcends the juvenile level for which many of these Mexican Gothics settle. The Faustian designs, sense of tragedy and Mango's jealousy of anyone who has more talent than him, makes the haunted musician a compelling figure. Magno is both gifted and cursed, yet he puts all his desire into crafting his protégé Laura into the world-famous pianist he should have become, but now never will. The sequence where he murders Alejandra in a jealous rage is gripping, and the fact that he hangs her portrait in his own living room in plain sight from his piano bench demonstrates his admiration for her talent. Sadly his tragic flaw does not allow him to accept the fact that she is his better. Such heightened dramatics add an operatic quality to the standard horror film formula, and such hyperbole makes *The Man and the Monster* special.

Monsters and Madmen
Movies: *Corridors of Blood* (3.0);
The Haunted Strangler (3.0);
The Atomic Submarine (3.0);
First Man Into Space (3.0)
Disc: 4.0
[Criterion Collection]

When I was a child back in the late 1950s and saw most of these movies

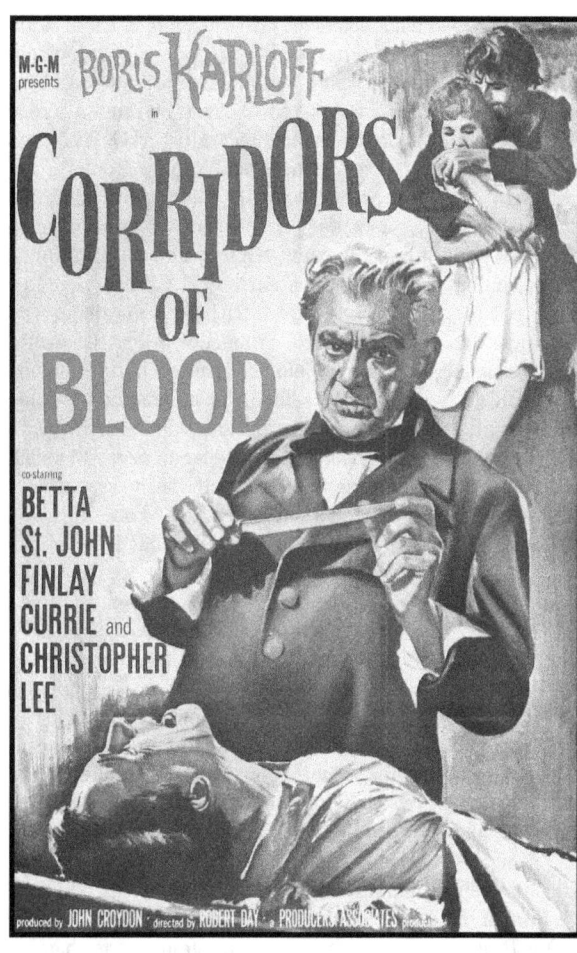

theatrically, I was impressed at their quality and professionalism. I never sensed that a connection existed between any of them as far as a common producer was concerned. I was never knowledgeable about Richard or Alex Gordon as entities until much later. While one can see Alex Gordon's credit on screen frequently, finding the name Richard Gordon is a much harder task. While I never associated with Alex personally except for a letter or two, Richard Gordon became a true ally of Midnight Marquee Press and of Gary and Susan specifically. At first being introduced to Richard through writer John R. Duvoli, who proposed a series of articles on the movies produced by Richard Gordon, I approached the affable elder Brit shyly to ask to borrow some photos and ad material, all of which Mr. Gordon, as I still think of him today, more than kindly consented. Dick Gordon was always friendly, offering a small correction here, a hint of advice there and his resources were always open to us. And not only that, Mr. Gordon became a huge supporter of all our published efforts, refusing any free copies and insisting he pay for oodles of our books and magazines. Even to this day Mr. Gordon sends us checks in support of our efforts and writes detailed, fact-filled letters of comment. Truly, a finer gentleman cannot be found. And modest as well. While he protects the marketing of all his projects like a proud parent and shrewd businessman, Mr. Gordon, on screen, hides his name behind production companies. But the legacy of Richard Gordon (and brother Alex with the inclusion of *The Atomic Submarine*) receives its just due with this box set (hopefully only the first and not the last!) produced to the highest technical expectations by Criterion. While the movies were issued originally by Image in excellent versions, Criterion treats these B productions as though they were Bergman or Hitchcock, each film undergoing slavish, pristine re-mastering and including extras galore. The list price might at first seem prohibitive, but seldom have science fiction, horror and monster movies of the 1950s- era been presented in such high-tech deluxe packages. These versions rival Criterion's stand-alone version of *Fiend Without a Face*, perhaps Richard Gordon's most recognized work, which was released several years ago.

First up is *The Haunted Strangler* (aka *Grip of the Strangler* in England), a quality low-budget production featuring a sensitive Boris Karloff performance. Under the guidance of Richard Gordon, who loved and respected the horror film icon, Gordon's productions starring Karloff would remain among the actor's finest work during the Boris' final decade. Director Robert Day mounts a fine production allowing Karloff the latitude to create a horrific psychopathic performance, depending only upon Karloff's ability to remove a dental bridge and contort his face, shoulders and fingers (without the use of horrifying makeup). Documentary extras explain that lack of budget led to the lack of makeup and Karloff's need to create a Mr. Hyde-style murderer using only his natural ability. But the truth remains that any cheesy makeup would have been far less successful than the method that acting genius Karloff employed here.

The movie opens with the hanging of the Haymarket Strangler 20 years earlier, and his autopsy and burial, handled by an attending physician, who collapses over the corpse, as the murderer's scalpel is thrown quickly into the coffin before it is sealed for burial. A generation later writer Jim Rankin (Karloff) is investigating the case, trying to prove that an innocent man was executed for the serial murders. When having the grave opened and finding the scalpel, Rankin transforms into the twisted fiend and the murders begin once again. Of course by the movie's end Karloff's actual identity is revealed to him by his own wife.

Even though the serial killer is referred to as the Haymarket Strangler, the fiend's method of operation is to first strangler the female victim with his good hand, and using the contorted second hand, the scalpel is used to slice and dice her and it is actually the stab wounds that result in the victim's death. Karloff as the distinguished Rankin is always smiling and has his full head of silver hair combed perfectly in place, high on his head. However, after his transformation into the Haymarket Strangler, when Rankin returns home to family and friends, his face is overtly worried with eyes darting from side to side, avoiding direct eye contact, and his hair is greasy and flattened. Yet no one suspects anything is seriously wrong.

Karloff's performance, with his grimaced face, sunk in mouth and contorted upper body remains us of a stroke victim, if it were not for Karloff's mobility and excessive energy. His quick transformation, once he clutches the killing knife, is fascinating to behold, and when he is almost caught in his altered identity at home, he places the knife on his library shelf and returns to his normal persona. Without doubt Karloff rises above any flaws of the production and screenplay and makes the audience notice only him. It is a transcendent performance and perhaps Karloff's finest during his last decade of acting. The film does suffer slightly from low-budget period sets (especially the prison and the prison graveyard, that simply cry out for more) and the movie does feature a slightly lethargic pace, but whenever Karloff is on screen, the movie holds our interest.

Extras include current on-screen interviews with director Robert Day and several cast members, who fondly remember being part of the production back in 1957-1958.

After the success of *The Haunted Strangler*, *Corridors of Blood* followed, originally called *Doctor of Seven Dials*. It was released in 1958 in England and a year later appeared in the U.S., double-billed (the lower-end yet) with *Werewolf in a Girl's Dormitory*, a foreign-dubbed werewolf schlocker. *Corridors of Blood*, a classy

historical drama with Gothic roots, deserved much better.

First, what makes *Corridors of Blood* shine is its all-star cast (Boris Karloff and Christopher Lee, two icons of horror, with handsome Hammer leading man Francis Matthews, and a stew of professional British character actors featuring Francis De Wolff, Basil Dignam, Frank Pettingell and Nigel Green, as well as a sexy supporting performance from young Yvonne Roman, here billed by Yvonne Warren). Secondly, the production used existing sets at MGM's British studios, making the production values shine for a lower-budgeted B movie. For such a period piece, the expansive sets (the medical building, surgical theater and the Seven Dials Tavern with side rooms) alone give the movie a black-and-white Hammer look.

The story concerns a robust Boris Karloff playing Doctor Thomas Bolton, a sympathetic surgeon known for the speed of his operations in the era before anesthesia was invented. Bolton, ridiculed by his peers, believes that by placing his patient into a deep sleep that surgical pain could be lessened. As the kindly doctor goes to the Seven Dials Tavern weekly to administer to the poor, he chastises one young woman, who forces her daughter to sell flowers on the street corner. He tells the mother that unless the girl stays off her feet for a few weeks, she might loose her leg, which is infected. He even gives the mother some coins to compensate her for financial loss during the recovery time. Meanwhile Bolton begins to experiment on himself by inhaling chemical mists created in his closet laboratory and he soon develops an addiction, becoming a hapless victim, used by the conniving criminal element at Seven Dials. In his stupor, he signs any number of death certificates for murder victims of so-called Resurrection Joe (Christopher Lee), who smothers unknowing victims brought to secret rooms by beautiful young women. The bodies can then be sold to local hospitals. It's a variation on Burke and Hare.

The film's dramatic center follows the committed Bolton as he tries to convince the authorities that anesthesia does in fact work, but every time he is given a surgical review, the patient awakens and goes ballistic and the review committee rejects his efforts. Only after his violent death at the hands of Resurrection Joe (who is burned by acid in a grisly climatic sequence) is Bolton proven to be a pioneer, when his son carries on and perfects the method.

Corridors of Blood is not a horror movie, although its Gothic set pieces and cast of characters reflect such horror roots. The movie is more a historic drama with sequences of murder, bloody surgeries and violent death provided by Christopher Lee, whose performance is mostly devoid of dialogue. For Richard Gordon, *Corridors of Blood* must have been a tough sell, being neither fish nor fowl. It was quite literally a *Curse of the Cat People* in a sea of *I Walk with a Zombie* and *Leopard Man*. But as presented here, the movie is solid entertainment all the way with an excellent Boris Karloff performance, again among the best of his latter day performances. Extras include a detailed letter from the Motion Picture Association of America noting the need for censorship cuts; audio commentary with Richard Gordon and Tom Weaver; current on screen interviews with director Robert Day, co-stars Francis Matthews and Yvonne Romain; still and production gallery and theatrical trailer. Seldom does such a small picture demand so many extras, but they alone are worth the price of admission.

In 1959 Richard Gordon and Amalgamated Productions left the world of Gothic Hammer-inspired horrors behind and embarked upon the commercially viable world of sci-fi monsters, with *First Man Into Space*, starring cult B-star mainstay Marshall Thompson as the all business military commander of the U.S. space mission. The British production added American Thompson for commercial appeal and the setting was New Mexico, approximated. As a child this movie thrilled me to death and I have fond memories of it; however, when seen today, the movie's juvenile trappings undermine the production slightly. First of all, our first man into space returns as a head-to-toe space tar corroded fiend with a tooth or two showing and one human eye protruding. When approaching people, he never walks when he can pounce and extends his arm, mummy-like, to slit their throats and feed on their blood. During the climax, when the fiend is being led to an atmospheric chamber that will help him breathe, our monster goes out of his way, even in a weakened state, to bash and shove every single piece of furniture he finds. Not that the furniture is in his way, but as a monster he is compelled to attack it.

The film's basic triangle is pure kid stuff. We have the commander (Thompson), slightly jealous of his younger brother (Lt. Dan Prescott), a test pilot that gets all the

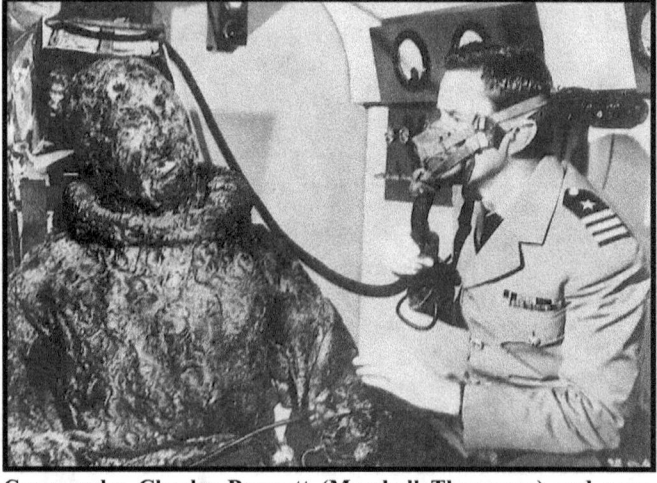

Commander Charles Prescott (Marshall Thompson) and monstrous brother Dan (Bill Edwards), from *First Man Into Space*.

action, adventure and beautiful women that the commander cannot. When Dan goes into space, the commander wants him to turn around and head back, but the dazed lieutenant defies his orders and continues venturing outward and outward, unfortunately crossing a meteor field of corrosive radiation, which seals his fate. Older brother Charles is all protocol, the following-orders type of guy. Younger Dan is more about the glitz and fame and the women that such fame will earn him. Enter sexpot Tia Francesca (Marla Landi), Dan's scientist girlfriend, and the other reason Charles is jealous of Dan. However, almost shockingly, by the movie's end, as Dan lies dying, ranting and raving about being the first man into space, older brother Charles walks alone down the corridor, grieving the death of his brother, Tia dries her tears and runs off down the hall after Charles, placing her arm smugly around his back. Even to kids back in 1959, we understood that Tia has already moved on and has romantic feelings for her beau's older brother. But she's moving a tad too rapidly, don't you think?

Like most of the science-fiction horror movies of this era, *First Man Into Space* has its slow sections, usually consisting of military men barking orders and trying to find rescued Dan usually in the arms of a beautiful woman. The sequences with the tar encrusted Dan lurking and hunting victims throughout the countryside are very moody and photographed effectively, but such sequences arrive later in the production when an air of lethargy has already entered. The film's climax as brother and brother are reunited and Charles risks his life to help Dan enter the atmospheric pressure chamber is very suspenseful and well done. Director Robert Day seems to have no problems in switching gears from Gothic horror to modern-day science fiction. If the film's pacing had been energized a tad, *First Man Into Space* would have been a first rate B production. As it now stands, it is perhaps second to the Gordon classic, *Fiend Without A Face*, which also starred Marshall Thompson, but *Fiend Without A Face* remains the superior movie, mostly because of its awesome flying brain creatures. Extras include the standard trailer, poster and still gallery, but as a special treat Robert Day is interviewed on screen, as is Marla Landi.

Finally brother Alex Gordon's *The Atomic Submarine* rounds out the box set, and the pressing here is again spectacular. *The Atomic Submarine*, claustrophobic and mostly limited to sequences aboard the submarine, manages to never bog down in tedium. Yes, the film is rather talky but the character conflict and interchanges always remain interesting. Of course the film builds up to the climactic sequence where the members of the submarine go aboard the underwater flying saucer and meet the furry one-eyed alien ruler, and while the execution of the beast is rather funky and low-budget, it still works with that booming voice and odd lighting effects (featuring minimalist sets that are also rendered effectively). Once the alien's eye is shot out and the oozing fluids drip down, all the kids in the matinee audience were screaming. Of course when the saucer attempts to dive out of the ocean waters and return to space, but is shot down, another round of screaming approval develops. *The Atomic Submarine* was never publicized as a true science fiction movie, but the idea to cross genres (remember, back in the late 1950s submarine movies were a big deal) was insightful. Working with a minimal budget, *The Atomic Submarine* delivers the goods. But the well-defined professional cast including Arthur Franz, Dick Foran, Brett Halsey, Tom Conway and others keep the non-action scenes interesting. And Joi Lansing is always nice to look at, playing a well-defined 1950s heroine.

It is a credit to Criterion that they re-mastered and presented all four of these movies in such a prestige presentation. The prints have never looked better and the extras are marvelous (including the interview with Brett Halsey). Richard Gordon and the late Alex Gordon should be smiling, knowing that their legacy of great science fiction movies has been preserved for the next generation of fantasy film aficionados.

Psycho
Movie: 3.5; Disc: 3.5
[Universal]

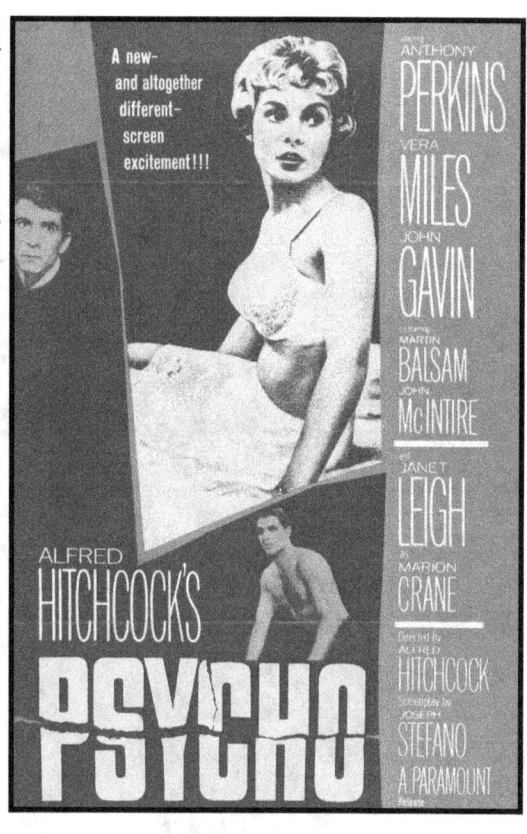

Alfred Hitchcock's *Psycho* is at heart a simple morality tale, told from diverse points of view. We have Marion Crane, the slinky office worker, who sneaks out to motel rooms during extended lunch breaks to make love with her divorced boyfriend, who states he cannot marry the sizzling woman until he makes more money and pays off his debts (how many women have heard such a story?). After she steals a client's money from the office (her boss tells her to place the cash in a safety deposit box) and runs away to join the object of her lust, she has a moral epiphany and decides to return the stolen cash, even scribbling a note of how much money she spent from the original stash and needs to replace. Lonely hotel manager Norman Bates, who shuns people, is a full-time caregiver for his grumpy, elderly mother (when asked whether he has any friends by Marion, Bates replies, "A boy's best friend is his mother."). Of course Bates both murdered and absorbed the psychological persona of his mother, and whenever sexual urges well up inside, the vengeful persona of mother emerges to dispatch perceived tramps to preserve the innocence of her son. A highway patrolman, wearing large dark shades, awakens Marion, who has fallen asleep alongside the road. After she is detained by the steely-eyed policeman, he lets her go and she finally drives off, but is followed for the longest time by the patrol car. Later in the day when Marion stops at a used car dealership to swap her old car for a new, the same patrol car appears across the street, and the policeman, leaning on a car, simply stares at her. He even pulls his car onto the lot when Marion finishes making her deal and drives off. The cop is dutifully suspicious, yet at the same time he seems threatening, overbearing and downright spooky. Private investigator Arbogast knows Marion stole $40,000, but the family hires him to get her back and return the money,

so to avoid legal involvement. He is driven by the allure of money, by the intellectual pursuit of his prey, and while he knows he should not go alone to the spooky house behind the Bates Motel, he is driven more by his obsession to succeed than by any outright sense of right and wrong. However, when in that daring overhead shot "Mrs." Bates emerges from the bedroom, the knife cocked above her shoulders, and Arbogast tumbles backward down the staircase, he gets a dose of morality, of the adage that curiosity killed the cat. He too, like Marion before him, ends up in the swamp.

Psycho is a detailed character study of several people, all broken, all conflicted, all motivated by some form of morality yet sidetracked by other lusts and drives. Hitchcock plays around and surprises us by killing off his repentant thief before she finishes her cleansing shower, washing away the sins of the past week. In that shower she does not find redemption or salvation, she only finds bloody death. And Norman Bates too is attracted sexually to the sensual Marion Crane, as is Sam Loomis (John Gavin), who enjoys his afternoon delight with the hot babe. Within Bate's psyche lurks the two components of morality, the avenging angel Mother and the lustful, peephole-motivated demon inside. When Marion's equally hot sister Lila (Vera Miles) finds the partially preserved corpse of Mother in the wine cellar, Norman's lust is again aroused. Bates becomes mother and tries to finish off Lila much in the same way he finished off Marion, but Sam Loomis comes to her rescue and Bates becomes locked in his Mother mode for eternity.

Psycho, like the best Hitchcocks, is twisted and deals with the kinks that all humans bear under the societal pressures of imposed morality. Made as a little black-and-white picture using his B production team that produced the weekly *Alfred Hitchcock Presents* TV series, *Psycho* succeeds because of its eccentricity and low-key ethics. The movie becomes classic by nature of its expert scripting and wonderful, in-depth performances, but the movie's moral universe features amplified human defects to which we all can relate. And therein lies the true success of *Psycho*.

**Forbidden Planet
[50th Anniversary
Two-Disc Special Edition]**
Movie: 3.0; Disc: 4.0
[Warner]

In many ways *Forbidden Planet* is an anomaly, a so-called science fiction classic from 1956 that is unlike any other movie of its era. In many ways the film's script, written by Cyril Hume, is very adult in nature, recycling Shakespeare's *The Tempest* for the popcorn trade and dealing with the complexities of monsters from the id. Yet, on the other hand, the script meanders with tons of concessions to the juvenile audience including the too cute Robby the Robot creating 60 gallons of whiskey for the cook and Dr. Morbius' daughter Altaira all simplistic innocence and pure sexuality, who praces around withwild animals wearing a very short skirt, legs and feet bare, and sometimes she even bathes nude to titillate the astronauts, who have been in hibernation for the past year and crave the contact of women. The backstory of the Krell civilization is more complex and given in such short spurts that it is difficult for even the adults in the audience to understand what exactly destroyed them. Dr. Morbius, the only survivor of his exploration crew and the only one of the crew that did not wish to return to Earth, is very aloof and mysterious. On the other hand, exploring spacemen Commander Adams, Lt. Farman and the cook are sometimes just plain silly and heroic in an annoying, broad manner. Many people mention that *Forbidden Planet* created the blueprint for the TV series *Star Trek*, and therein lies the strengths and weakness of the movie.

Besides the flaws mentioned above, other flaws include the film's focusing too heavily on the stunning state of the art visual effects. Morbius parades around his complex demonstrating all the technology that exists in his world, everything from a man-serving robot to protective steel panels that appear to protect that world. We spend plenty of time watching the saucer-ship land on the alien landscape, plenty of time watching Robby the Robot cart the visitors across the alien desert, plenty of time watching Altaira tame even the wildest of beasts, plenty of time viewing comic relief sequences, plenty of time exploring the last vestiges of the Krell civilization, etc. When it comes to the psychic demons created by Morbius and the cartoonish attack of the Id monster, such true drama appeals to get short shrift and the monster attacks are too few and far between.

Basically, *Forbidden Planet* does not know whether it wants to be a deep psychologically motivated adult sci-fi drama and play to the serious trade, or, whether it wants to be a special effects lark and pander to the children, who are awed by the futuristic planetscapes, futuristic technology and the amazing plaything called Robby. Director Fred M. Wilcox plays it safe, tries to be both, and *Forbidden Planet* ultimately suffers from a split personality.

Seldom has a major studio pumped so much money into a genre production, especially during the drive-in era of the 1950s. For producing a science fiction monster movie with such glossy and expensive production values, we should all be grateful. The use of CinemaScope and color is breathtaking for its time, and the film, as represented here, is truly a visual delight. However, it seems the dramatic aspects are sacrificed to attract the juvenile trade and commerce triumphs over art (remember, the studio had a large overhead to recoup!).

The two-disc special edition is a treasure-trove of delights, including an episode of TV's *The Thin Man* starring Robby the Robot, and the entire feature film *The Invisible Boy* that starred Robby the Robot in a science fiction adventure film that totally veers over to the side of juvenile entertainment. The package includes marvelous outtakes, three documentaries, trailers and excerpts from the *MGM on Parade* TV series. But most of all, the re-mastered print even surpasses the original laser disc release from the Criterion Collection. Simply stated, *Forbidden Planet* never looked better. But is looking better good enough?

Do You like Hitchcock?
Movie: 3.5; Disc: 3.5
[Anchor Bay]

For me, Dario Argento is the greatest horror film director of the past 40 years, surpassing the careers of peers such as George Romero, John Carpenter, Tobe Hooper and Wes Craven. While Argento's art reveals the director to seem to be deeply disturbed, his flair for visual story-telling and visceral direction makes him the master of his domain. While Argento's most recent work (such as *The Card Player*) is superior to most, it remains inferior to his best, movies such as *Deep Red* and *Suspiria*. However, Argento's 2005 made-for-TV feature film, *Do You Like Hitchcock*, simply takes the maestro in an entirely new direction.

Italian TV does not face the censorship problems that hamper artistic expression on American TV, but *Do You Like Hitchcock?* is rather tame stylistically for Argento. Yes, the film features some heated nudity and lovemaking, but the violence is very much toned down, and perhaps this more mainstream approach benefits Argento at this stage in his career. Argento, who with Mario Bava created the giallo sub-genre, always gave props to Alfred Hitchcock for being one of his major inspirations, and here, with this love letter to Hitch, Argento creates a playful homage to his master that may be Argento's best movie in a generation. Toned down splatter only means Argento can concentrate on his keen visual eye and create set pieces that rival his best early classics.

The story is deceptively simple. A young college student, geeky in appearance, is writing his dissertation on German Expressionistic cinema and watches the same films that his viewing audience knows and loves. Of course his love for movies extends to Hitchcock, and this young man, Giulio, frequents his local mom-and-pop DVD shop, owned and managed by an equally film-obsessed man, Andrea. Into the shop comes young and sexy Sasha, a single hottie who lives in the plaza across from Giulio's apartment, a seeming Euro updating of the similar open-apartment views provided in Hitchcock's *Rear Window*. Of course the horny young man uses binoculars to watch Sasha in various phrases of undress, and she is aware of the voyeur's carnal interest in her. Sasha, a brunette, befriends an equally sizzling blonde at the video shop, and both express interest in wanting to rent Hitchcock's *Strangers on a Train*. The plot of *Strangers on a Train* involves two strangers who agree to murder someone for each other, using their just-having-met status as the perfect excuse of getting away with murder. Before long the girls appear to be very close, sitting outside and touching one another in a sexually suggestive (yet subtle) manner. Sasha lives with her mother, an overbearing bitch, and before long a stranger uses a key to enter Sasha's apartment to murder the mother, bashing her head in with a metal object. And Giulio figures that Sasha and her blonde buddy Federica are in cahoots and that Sasha must return the favor by murdering someone that Federica wants dead. So the video geek follows Federica around town, jeopardizing his relationship with girlfriend Arianna, who thinks he is obsessed, paranoid and losing touch with reality.

Ah, but it's the visuals that carry the movie. Amazingly, sometimes it appears that Argento is mimicking the visual style of early Brian De Palma, who himself was paying tribute to Hitchcock in films such as *Sisters, Dressed to Kill, Obsession, Body Double*, etc. In fact, when the mother dies, the dying woman uses her hand to smear her blood all over her apartment window, her outstretched hand sliding down the windowpane, leaving a trail of blood. A similar sequence occurred in De Palma's *Sisters*. Also the climactic scene involves the unknown murderer meandering around near the top of a large staircase at the glass-framed apartment complex across from Giulio's apartment. Because of the glass structure, we can see when Giuio's girl friend stupidly, alone, runs across the street to climb those stairs to catch the fiend, and we see when the lone police detective arrives at the scene, and he too climbs the stairs. The sequence reminds audiences of similar sequences from early Argento movies, and

such visuals are also suggestive of De Palma at his best. Of course, Giulio is incapacitated with a broken foot and he wears a heavy plaster cast, suggesting James Steward from *Rear Window*. Our hero can only watch from the safe confines of his own apartment as his girlfriend and detective try to apprehend the fiend.

In one of the film's best sequences, Giulio breaks his foot leaping down from spying at a window where he observes Federica's boss demand sexual favors for his agreeing to be quiet about her stealing money form the company. Giulio, who rides a moped, breaks his foot and hobbles desperately to the safe confines of his bike as the bald and ferocious pursuer runs down the eerily illuminated night-lit streets screaming, "I will kill you!" Giulio manages to mount his moped, sputter off down the street, only to spinout and fall, writhing in pain. The money shot is when the obsessed boss, arm outstretched, comes within inches of grabbing Giulio, only to have the moped burst to freedom at the last possible second.

In the best Hitchcock sense, the climax involves a victim hanging on to dear life (she tells her saviors to let her go) by hanging over the side of a roof, the drain pipe falling apart, as two people try to grab and hold on to her. A similar sequence occurred in *Vertigo*.

And the third superior sequence occurs as Giulio is attacked by a friend and thrust into a fully-filled bathtub (sorry, not a shower in sight), where the assailant tries to drown the unwary victim by submerging his head as he kicks and splashes. It's a wonderful sequence.

Do You Like Hitchcock? suffers a few lapses in pacing, briefly, but otherwise is

a marvelous Hitchcock-inspired homage that offers peak suspense and thrills and maintains Dario Argento's superb visual eye. Once again, if Dario Argento never made another film (and let's hope he makes many more), this film would be a proper coda to a long and fascinating cinematic career. It's a movie that forces audiences to jump and hide behind finger-covered eyes, but it also makes audiences smile. We are being manipulated by a master and enjoy every aspect of the ride.

Scant extras include an Italian language behind-the-scenes making of documentary, an Argento bio and trailer.

The Death of Poe
Movie: 2.5; Disc: 3.5
[Alpha New Cinema]

Baltimore stage and film actor Mark Redfield made the decision long ago to become a large fish in a small pond, by remaining true to his hometown roots. Instead of exploring the largest New York or West Coast acting arena and most likely sustaining a journeyman career doing character work on stage and in film, Redfield became an auteur, co-scripting, directing, designing and starring in small self-made productions. Redfield's last major movie was *Dr. Jekyll and Mr. Hyde*, a wonderful little film that paid tribute to Hammer. This time out, *The Death of Poe* is a much more intimate and minimalist production, almost becoming an art film for the horror chic. And it becomes a film of merit.

Interestingly, Redfield crafts *The Death of Poe* as a reflection of his own life, a metaphor for any struggling auteur filmmaker who does it all, including raising the finances for his art. Redfield, in the interesting making-of documentary that accompanies the feature, stresses several times that his movie is not a Poe biography. Instead, the film is a fevered look at the last week of Poe's life, told mostly subjectively from the frenzied brain of the tortured, sickly artist, as he lengthens his quick pass through Baltimore to tap three potential investors, who might invest in his proposed literary arts magazine that he hopes to publish and edit (instead of remaining an editor-for-hire of other people's journals). During the middle section of the movie, Poe meets and greets these generally pompous moneybags and gives them the glad hand, superficial smile and pitch. The first potential investors are the Wainwright twins (portrayed masterfully by perennial Baltimore actor George Stover, in a split-screen dual role performance), the first of which is anxious to contribute funds as long as the name of the journal is changed to *The Wainwright Journal*. However, the grizzled Scrooge counterpart twin is adamant in his refusal to allow his brother to give a cent to such a foolish enterprise. The second investor is just as bad, implying he will give money only if Poe publishes his daughter's embarrassingly bad poetry. Poe is left speechless. By the third meeting, Poe is ill and lethargic, as his pitch looses its zip and he succumbs to begging for the money.

Eating in a pub later that night, mindful of his promise to his late wife Virginia not to drink alcohol, Poe is joined by two old chums that he remembers from his days at the military academy. They seem happy to see him but insist he drink, and once he downs one drink, he quickly follows through with more, soon giving these strangers his rehearsed pitch for funding, regrettably mentioning that he has already raised $1,000 in cash. After Poe stumbles out of the tavern, his former friends attack and rob him of his cash, leaving him drunk and disoriented in the gutters of Baltimore.

For Redfield, such investor's pitches become a necessary evil in the world of producing independent films. Compromise upon compromise has to be made, since investors want something for themselves in exchange for investing their cash. And in Redfield's vision, such potential investors become predators who beat and rob the artist, leaving them for dead in the gutter. In the last week of Edgar Allan Poe's life, perhaps Mark Redfield sees his own life more favorably as the artist as victim metaphor.

Other than Redfield's quite masterful performance as Poe (both as the gentleman artist and as the rapidly-declining victim of dementia), the major success of the production belongs to cinematographer Jeff Herberger, who contributes all the compositing matte work that allows live actors to be superimposed over miniatures and still photographs, to create Poe's Baltimore on a budget. Herberger's cinematography, rich in black-and-white tones, with plenty of shadows, creates the permeating malevolent mood necessary for the production to grab the viewer. As Poe becomes delirious and is dying, more and more of his frantic visions and nightmares invade the screen, in snatches of blinding color. As the film races to an inevitable conclusion, the dream sequences become more invasive and more complex, featuring layer upon layer of imagery, all masterfully concocted by Herberger. Also, Jennifer Rouse's stark musical score must be noted, and it greatly complements the visuals created by the cinematography.

Interesting enough, the film ends as a continuous loop with the very same images that begin the film: the naked body of Poe worked over by a mortician on a bare table, that segment melding into one of the fully dressed Poe, in death, lying on that same table, with that segment transforming into Poe's wooden coffin now lying on that very same table. A montage of the casket being buried and a newspaper reporter writing up a story of Poe's death both begins and ends the movie. Such a frame suggests that the entire story may have occurred within Poe's fevered brain as he lies dying, or, the frame might simply be an external narrative that starts at the point of Poe's death and retraces the events, during the final week, that lead up to such tragedy.

Performances, many delivered by stage actors whose broad performances suit the style of the equally theatrical style movie, shine. Kevin Shinnick (the current publisher of *Scarlet* magazine) plays the dedicated doctor trying to save Poe, and Redfield company player Jennifer Rouse shines as his comforting assistant. Production coordinator Wayne Shipley plays one of Poe's relatives, a man more concerned over who is obligated to pay the $7 hospital fee than concerned about the life of his nephew. The ensemble cast more than rises to the occasion.

This affordably priced three-disc set features two silent movies based upon the works of Poe, a making of documentary, featurettes on the Poe house here in Baltimore and Poe's Baltimore, as well audio commentaries. Alpha New Cinema has created a stunning little package in which to promote *The Death of Poe*, a wonderfully realized Baltimore indepdendent film.

www.ingramcontent.com/pod-product-compliance
Lightning Source LLC
Chambersburg PA
CBHW080024130526
44591CB00036B/2637